teenMakeup

LOOKS TO MATCH YOUR EVERY MOOD

LINDA MASON

WATSON-GUPTILL PUBLICATIONS / NEW YORK

This book is for my beautiful, darling Daisy and for all daughters. Thank you for the inspiration and love you give us. I hope you keep your uninhibited, creative spark alight forever.

Senior Acquisitions Editor: Julie Mazur
Editor: Elizabeth Wright
Design (cover and interior): Margo Mooney
Production Manager: Barbara Greenberg

First published in 2004 by Watson-Guptill Publications,
a division of VNU Business Media, Inc.,
770 Broadway, New York, NY 10003
www.wgpub.com

Library of Congress Cataloging-in-Publication Data is available from the Library of Congress.

ISBN: 0-8230-2980-8

Printed in China

First printing, 2004

3 4 5 6 7 8 9 / 12 11 10 09 08 07 06 05

CONTENTS

acknowledgments   4

preface   5

about this book   6

the facts about modeling   8

MAKEUP 101:

THE BASICS   14

skin care   16

tools and techniques   24

using color   34

MAKEUP

STAR POWER   118

CAPRICORN   120

AQUARIUS   122

PISCES   124

ARIES   126

TAURUS   128

acknowledgments

This book has given me the opportunity to get to know Daisy's friends better and to meet my friends' and clients' daughters, such as Lindzay, the daughter of my neighbor, whom I have watched grow from a cute little baby into a beautiful young woman. I met Lucinda on a photo shoot. Another of the models, Caitlin (Pisces), is a graduate of a great beauty school in Greensboro, North Carolina, run by an incredible woman and friend, Parker Washburn.

Some special clients who just happened to walk into my shop one day looking great: Esra, Ming, and Alex.

I would like to thank my daughter Daisy for her help with the models and writing for this book. My thanks to all the great models who gave of their time to help me on this project: Alex Tatarsky, Alice Hlidek, Aziza Dyer, Caitlin Venters, Candice Duffy, Daisy Mason, Elizabeth Kadernauth, Elizabeth Cohn, Emma Messing Alabaster, Esra Padgett, Jennifer Sanoh, Jessica Sanoh, Katrina Lencek-Inagaki, Laura Stubben, Lindzay Wanner, Lucinda Ruh, Melissa Day, Ming Lin, Malaya Wibmer, Marcella Tosi, Natalie Gelman, Sasha Cohen, Sarah Yagerman, Sarah Levine, Shantie Midnight, Skye Fischer, Stephanie Schonbrun, Suzanne Brancaccio, and Tania Haselwander.

I would also like to thank the makeup artists who were once my students and interns: Heather Gould-Sale, Jessica Ross (for the makeup on Glamorous Tania); Tiffany French (for the makeup on Laura the Leo); Yuka Suzuki (for the makeup on Melissa the Sagittarius and Ming); Mimi Latham (for the makeup on Retro Suzanne, Glamorous Jennifer, Classic Tania, and Caitlin the Pisces); Nikki Berryman (for the makeup on Glamorous Jessica, Cool Jennifer, Prom Jennifer, Way-out-rageous Daisy, and Natalie); Nina Allen (for the way-out-rageous makeup on her beautiful daughter, Tania); Elise Kull (for the makeup on Cool Katrina and Retro Katrina); and Megan Belz (for the makeup on Glamorous Suzanne). My thanks to Utta, the hairstylist from the John Sahag Workshop (for the hair on Cool Katrina, Retro Katrina, and Glamorous Suzanne); Lynn Midolo (for the hair on Retro Suzanne, Marcella the Virgo, Caitlin the Pisces); and Eddie Teboul of L'Atelier New York (for the hair on Melissa the Sagittarius and Lauren the Leo). Last but not least, I want to thank Julie Mazur for entrusting me with this project; Elizabeth Wright for doing such a great job making this book more teen-accessible (as always, it's such a pleasure working with you!); Margo Mooney for her fabulous design; and Ellen Greene and Barbara Greenberg for their crucial contributions. Special thanks go to my agent, Jayne Rockmill, for all her zealous energy and expertise.

Daisy and Linda
Photo by Lorraine Sylvestre

Katrina, Sasha, and Daisy at elementary school graduation

preface

For the past twenty-five years, my work as a makeup artist has led me to work with teens—many as young as fourteen and fifteen. I work frequently with *Seventeen* and *YM*, but even on photo shoots for *Vogue* I have made up girls as young as fourteen.

I was crazy about makeup when I was a teen. I loved being able to transform myself—becoming a makeup artist and transforming others was just a continuation of this passion, and I love it. My daughter, Daisy, has always loved makeup and has enjoyed accompanying me on photo shoots and playing with makeup ever since she was a baby. When she was ten, she inspired me to create a makeup line using her drawings and my own drawings of her as the packaging.

Now a teenager, Daisy has inspired me to do this book. This book is for her friends (the girls you'll see being transformed throughout these pages), for her, and for all the teens out there. I want them to be able to enjoy the fun, creative aspect of makeup and experience the glamorous aspects of being a model without actually living through the hassles of the business.

Life is a journey of self-discovery, and your teen years are an especially important part of that journey. Teens love to express how they feel on the inside through the way they look on the outside. Trying out different images is a part of self-discovery—take time to play and experiment! This book will teach you how to express your sense of style with makeup. You don't have to stick with any one look—figuring out who you are is a process that takes time—usually forever! And that's okay. Going through a variety of different looks can help you understand how to make the most of your best qualities, and the sense of play can help strengthen your sense of who you are. At home, in front of your mirror, you can put on a punk face to express your wilder side, or wear a sweet look to soften your face and show a more innocent side of yourself.

Makeup is not just the ultimate fashion accessory—it can also be an art form! The more you experiment, the more you enjoy yourself, and the better you get at using it. Want to look more cool or more glamorous? Once you learn a few basic things about color, techniques, and tools, it's easy! Practice alone and surprise your friends with a new style, or go through this book and practice together. Makeup is all about transformation, so remember, you're never too old to play dress-up.

The Facts about **Modeling**

Are you crazy about makeup and hairstyles? Do you spend all of your allowance on fashion magazines? Do you have more outfits than Sarah Jessica Parker? Do you love being in the spotlight? If so, you have probably also fantasized about what it would be like to be a model. It may seem like a dream job, and for many girls it is, but there are some facts you should consider before you pursue modeling as a career (or hobby).

Modeling can be lots of fun, but you have to be very tough and able to distance yourself from your image. A strong sense of self-worth is critical. You cannot please everyone all the time—and some days you won't please anyone at all. Many girls are beautiful in real life, but they may not photograph well, or they might be too small, too tall, or they might not have the right "look for the moment."

If it's the money you are interested in, know that very few models earn a lot—only the big names you read about earn big bucks. If you count the time it takes to go on lots of appointments—when only a few will lead to actual work—and the cost of keeping a portfolio up to date, most teen models end up making about the same amount that they would at a summer job at the mall, if even that!

The fashion world is trendy, and a career in modeling is usually short. If you're interested in working as a model, you should also plan to attend and finish college so that you can get a good education and build a strong future after modeling.

the **FUN** PART

* Getting to wear fabulous clothes and accessories
* Working with talented, creative people
* Having an opportunity to learn an incredible amount in a short period of time
* Traveling to really cool places
* Meeting and developing a camaraderie with other models
* Learning to work as part of a team
* Getting lots of attention

the **HarD** PART

* Working during your vacations from school
* Always being judged on your physical appearance
* Having to wait until the last minute to know what you will be doing the next day
* Making an endless number of visits (called "go sees") to prospective clients before even getting hired for one job
* Getting to your job at 8 AM and having to wait until 4 PM to do your first

Alice modeling a glamorous look for a photo shoot

Alice with outrageous, freestyle makeup

Alice with cool makeup

Alice with retro makeup

The **Girls** in This **Book**

All the girls in this book are real, everyday teens like you. My teenage daughter, Daisy, inspired me to write this book, so instead of hiring professional models, I decided to use Daisy and her wonderful group of friends (as well as the daughters of some of my own friends) in the photographs. As you will see, they represent all different skin tones, hair colors, ethnic backgrounds, and personalities. You will see how different kinds of makeup can bring out many different qualities in a face and make the same face look dramatically different. Here, you see the girls without any makeup at all: flip through the book to find pictures of the girls wearing different makeup styles (you'll find page numbers for all the photos in the index on p. 144) .

alex t. Age 14

Favorite beauty tip Don't overdo the foundation! Natural is best. **Makeup must-have** Lip gloss—the fruitier and yummier the better! **Beauty role model** I think that Norah Jones always looks effortlessly fabulous. **Beauty party trick** Dusting subtle body shimmer on my cheeks and shoulders for a warm honey glow.

alice Age 18 **Favorite**

beauty tip Create unique eye shadow colors by layering a dark color first and then adding a light, shimmery color on top. **Makeup must-haves** Concealer with SPF 10 and glimmer dust. **Beauty role model** Brooke Shields. **Beauty party trick** I line my eyes with black eyeliner and eye shadow and use shimmery blue, pink, and silver gel eye shadows. On my lips, I use pale pink lip gloss. I also use bronzer to give my cheeks a fake tan look.

aziza Age 17

Favorite beauty tip Metallic soft blue eye shadow to bring out the eyes. **Makeup must-have** Cocoa butter. **Beauty role model** James King. **Beauty party trick** Colorful eyeliner applied under the eye and pretty blush.

caitlin Age 21

Favorite beauty tip Check the color of your foundation in the daylight to make sure it matches your neck. **Makeup must-have** Mascara. **Beauty role model** My mother, whose simple beauty tricks and rules like "take your makeup off before you go to bed" have stuck with me. **Beauty party trick** Dramatic eyes.

candice Age 18

Favorite beauty tip I put base on my lips to neutralize the color and make my lipstick last. **Makeup must-have** Mascara! **Beauty role model** My mom. **Beauty party trick** Using clear lip gloss as eye shadow or underneath eye shadow. I put it just under my brow.

daisy Age 17
Favorite beauty tip Using "cloud" eye shadow (white with a touch of lilac) to brighten my eyes and face. **Makeup must-haves** Blush and almond oil **Beauty role model** My mum. **Beauty party trick** Using liquid

elizabeth c.

Age 16 **Makeup must-haves** Concealer and lip gloss. **Beauty role model** Jennifer Aniston has great hair.

elizabeth k.

Age 19 **Favorite beauty tip** Bronzer works to highlight and accentuate your cheekbones, and adds dimensional glow to your face. **Makeup must-haves** Cleanser and a good moisturizer. **Beauty role model** Charlize Theron—she always looks elegant and flawless. She has great eyes and her makeup always coordinates with her attire. **Beauty party trick** Wearing lip gloss with a pearlized lipstick layered on top. It helps lips look full and inviting.

emma **Age** 17

Favorite beauty tip Avocado face masks. **Makeup must-have** Lip gloss. **Beauty role model** Drew Barrymore. **Beauty party trick** Using a colorful eyeliner.

esra **Age** 15 **Favorite**

beauty tip Natural-looking lip gloss is really easy to use and looks nice without being too fancy. **Makeup must-have** Glitter eyeliner—I wear it almost every day. The glitter spreads all around my eyes and makes them shimmer even after the liner has worn off. **Beauty role model** Edie Sedgewick. **Beauty party trick** Wearing makeup or clothes with more color and excitement than what you

jennifer **Age** 18

Favorite beauty tip If you're going to a party or other event and want your makeup to last, spray hair spray gently into the air and walk into the mist—your makeup will last all night. **Makeup must-have** Lip gloss. **Beauty role model** Iman—she has a beautiful personality and that beauty shows through in her physical appearance. **Beauty party trick** Applying makeup using natural light from your window.

jessica **Age** 18

Favorite beauty tip Apply makeup using natural light from your window. **Makeup must-have** lip gloss **Beauty role models** The model Iman, the actress Halle Berry, and the singers Brandy and Beyonce Knowles. **Beauty party trick** (same as Jennifer's, above)

katrina **Age** 17

Favorite beauty tip I'm a concealer junkie. I never leave the house without it under my eyes. **Makeup must-have** Cetaphil, for washing my face. I have very sensitive skin, and I use it twice a day, in the morning and at night. **Beauty role model** No one specific—just those girls who roll out of bed and are naturally beautiful. **Beauty party trick** Putting a smudge of black pencil eyeliner over my eye.

laura **Age** 19 **Favorite**

beauty tip Apply moisturizer directly after showering so your skin absorbs it better. **Makeup must-have** Green eyeliner. **Beauty role model** Kevin Aucoin (the late makeup artist). **Beauty party trick** Using a clear lip gloss to

lindzay Age 13

Favorite beauty tip My concept of beauty is feeling good about the way you look and trying out different styles. **Beauty role models** Audrey Hepburn, Catherine Zeta Jones, Katherine Hepburn, and Judy Garland.

lucinda Age 24

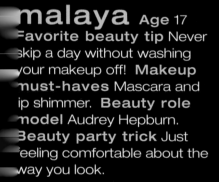

Favorite beauty tip Use purple or pink eye shadow to make green or blue eyes pop. I also like tinted purple lip gloss, purple mascara, and cute pink or orange blush. **Makeup must-haves** Lip gloss, blush, and a good night's sleep. **Beauty role models** Cameron Diaz, Christy Turlington, Charlize Theron, and Reese Witherspoon. **Beauty party trick** Smile, and use an eyelash curler and mascara. Also, put a shimmery light pink or gold in the inner corners of the eyes.

malaya Age 17

Favorite beauty tip Never skip a day without washing your makeup off! **Makeup must-haves** Mascara and lip shimmer. **Beauty role model** Audrey Hepburn. **Beauty party trick** Just feeling comfortable about the way you look.

marcella Age 18

Favorite beauty tip Less is more—go natural. **Makeup must-have** Foundation. **Beauty role model** Salma Hayek. **Beauty party trick** Eye shadow! It's colorful (I like purple or blue) and brings emphasis to the eyes. A change from the norm. Fun to mix it up; people notice the difference.

melissa Age 21

Favorite beauty tip Using warm colors of blush with cool shades of eye makeup. **Makeup must-have** Lip gloss. **Beauty role model** Kim Basinger. **Beauty party trick** Orange-tinted lip color.

ming Age 15

Makeup must-have Black eyeliner. **Beauty role model** Bjork—she's so unique and creative. **Beauty party trick** Drawing a star under the eye with black eye pencil.

natalie Age 18

Favorite beauty tip Hold the mascara wand a few seconds on the ends of your lashes to set the curl. **Makeup must-haves** Mascara, tinted lip gloss, and moisturizer. **Beauty role model** My friend Daisy. If I see something interesting on someone, I will try it. **Beauty party trick** Putting shimmer or glitter in my eyebrow arch and on my cheekbones. I also like to wear fake tattoos and rhinestone tattoos, or a unique color of eye shadow to make party makeup special.

sarah l. Age 17

Favorite beauty tip Don't overload your skin. I like to wear eye makeup with just lip gloss, or lipstick and no eye shadow. **Makeup must-have** Chapstick. **Beauty role model** Ginger Rogers. **Beauty party trick** Metallic shimmer.

sarah y. Age 18

Favorite beauty tip Using a light pink gloss to tone down my lips and accentuate my other features. **Makeup must-have** Mascara. **Beauty role model** My big sister, Rebecca. **Beauty party trick** Go darker on the eye makeup and have fun with colors.

sasha Age 17

Favorite beauty tip Using lip gloss on my eyes. **Makeup must-have** Lip gloss. **Beauty role model** Besides Linda Mason, Naomi Campbell because she is just so beautiful. **Beauty party trick** Applying lip gloss on lids and then eye shadow over it.

sky Age 14

Favorite beauty tip Bring out the color of your eyes by using colored eye pencil. **Makeup must-have** Mascara. **Beauty role model** I love the way Giselle makes everything looks so natural! **Beauty party trick** Parties love shine!

stephanie Age 15

Favorite beauty tip Using a light shimmer on the eyes. **Makeup must-haves** Mascara to elongate my lashes. **Beauty role models** Paulina Poriskova, Jennifer Lopez, Elizabeth Hurley, and Tyra Banks. **Beauty party trick** Using black liner on the outer half of the top lid with a light gold or green shimmer eye shadow and a neutral lip gloss.

suzanne b. Age 17

Favorite beauty tip Bright colored eye shadows to bring out the eyes. **Makeup must-have** Mascara. **Beauty role model** Kate Moss. **Beauty party trick** Dark lipstick.

tania Age 18

Favorite beauty tip Brighten your face by wearing cream blush and mascara. **Makeup must-haves** After washing my face I always apply vitamin E. **Beauty role model** My mom. **Beauty party trick** I don't need one—my mom took lessons from Linda Mason, and now she always does my makeup!

MakeUP
101: THE BASICS

Before you learn about different styles of makeup, you need to know some basics. Welcome to Makeup 101! In this section, I will teach you how to take care of your skin so that you look super—even with a bare face. Then I will answer all your questions about makeup: what to buy (powder? pencil? matte? sheer?), where to put it, and how to apply it. Finally, I'll explain how to mix and match makeup colors to bring out the "bling" in your beautiful face!

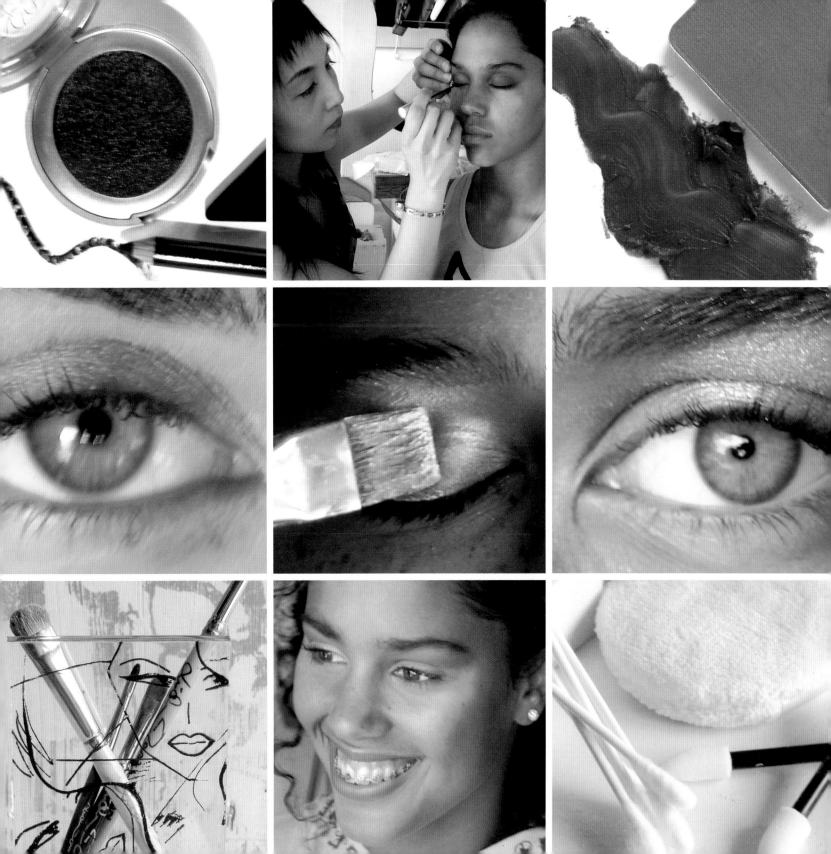

skin care

Have you ever had to deal with a big blemish on the day you were supposed to have your yearbook picture taken? Let's face it, teenage **skin** is moody, and taking care of it can seem like a full-time job. Here's the good news: you can minimize the conditions that cause the two biggest teen skin problems—blocked pores and pimples—if you learn good skin-care habits. That doesn't mean slathering on pimple medication or harsh astringents that dry out your skin (a common teen skin-care mistake). **Good habits** prevent problems *before* they start and give you a **healthy glow** so you'll look like a **cover girl** in all your yearbook pictures!

Cleansing

During the day, your skin is exposed to all the dirt and pollution in the air; overnight, as you sleep, your skin is getting rid of waste. So it is very important to cleanse your skin in the morning *and* in the evening.

The best soap is one that cleans naturally and gently and that you can use twice a day without making your skin too dry. If your skin is normal or dry, I recommend a natural aloe vera soap because it's gentle and moisturizing. Natural tea tree oil soap is best if you have pimples and blackheads. If you have ultrasensitive skin, avoid soap and use a gentle cleanser instead (see "Cleansers and Toners" on p. 19).

**Aloe vera soap
for dry skin**

**Tea tree oil soap
for oily skin**

Don't forget to massage your nose when you are cleansing! Rub your fingers over your nose lightly when your face is dry. Is the skin there rougher than it is on the rest of your face? Can you feel the blocked pores? Don't think that you have to "dry up" the area to solve the problem. All you have to do is cleanse it really well. Rinse your face with warm—not hot— water, and massage your skin lightly with soap. Pay special attention to the nose and spend at least ten seconds massaging it in a circular motion with your two middle fingers. Your chin may need the same extra attention. It's a good idea to use a gentle facial scrub from time to time as well—once every two weeks is usually often enough.

cleansers and TONERS

If you wear a cream foundation or base during the day, use a cleanser and toner at night and only use soap in the morning—cleanser dissolves foundation better than soap does. If you have dry skin, use a cream cleanser; if you have oily skin, a foam or gel cleanser is best. Massage your face lightly with the cleanser as you would with soap. Pay extra attention to the nose, chin, and forehead. A cotton ball soaked in a gentle toner will remove any remaining traces of dirt or cleanser (if the cotton ball is too dry, it will irritate your skin). You may be tempted to wipe out that oil with a strong toner, but don't do it! Strong toner can irritate and over-dry oily skin, making it secrete even more oil! A gentle formula is better. If your skin is pretty sensitive, don't use soap on it at all. Instead, use an extremely gentle cleanser and toner in the morning and at night.

MOISTURIZERS

If you have dry skin, smooth on a lightweight, daytime moisturizer after you wash your face. Some moisturizers have UV protection, which is a great way to cover two bases at once! If you have oily skin, you don't really need moisturizer. Just make sure you drink lots of water and are careful not to use too many products that dry out your skin.

Skin Problems

Most teens have skin problems occasionally, if not all the time. In your teen years, your hormone balance is changing, and that causes your skin to produce more oil at certain times than it does at others. A healthy diet and good skin-care habits are essential to dealing with the ups and downs in your hormone levels and their effects on your skin. *Drink lots of water and eat lots of fresh salad, fruits, and vegetables!* Don't eat food cooked in a lot of fat, or large amounts of cheese or sugar.

Teen skin is super sensitive—it will show any inner conflict you may be having, and it can react instantaneously to things that come in contact with it. Touching your face with your hands during the day can spread pimples like wildfire. Even hair products can cause pimples around the face. If your hair falls on your face and you are plagued with pimples in that area, your hair products may be causing them. If you suspect this is happening, don't use your conditioner for a couple weeks to see if your skin improves. If it doesn't, try changing your shampoo and wearing your hair off your face.

Special pimple creams and medications are meant to be used just on the pimple itself, otherwise they can dry and irritate healthy skin. It sounds a little odd, but if an area of your face is overly dry from acne cream, massaging that area with natural almond oil and leaving it on for a while before cleansing your skin will help heal the flaky skin or scars caused by popping pimples and drying them with ointment. (For tips on hiding zits with concealer, see p. 27.)

facial MASKS

Use a mud mask from time to time to deep-cleanse your pores and exfoliate dead skin cells. (Exfoliation is the process of removing the dull, dead cells from your skin's top layer.) There are also nourishing and moisturizing masks for those of you with dryer skin. Facial masks can be fun to do on a sleepover with other beauty treatments, but keep in mind that no two skins are alike. Find the best regime for yourself and change it when necessary.

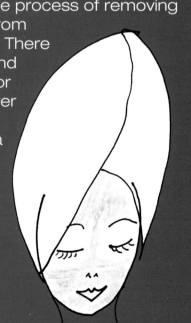

PROBLEM areas

Your Nose The nose is naturally oily, and most of us tend not to pamper it as much as we do the rest of our skin, so the area stays rougher, and the pores can become blocked and cause blackheads. All this makes your base/foundation look heavier when you apply it to the area. You can buy pore-cleansing strips at most drugstores; these are great for getting at the dirt that causes blackheads. Don't use them too often because they can irritate your skin.

Your Chin This area is also very prone to oiliness, blackheads, and pimples. It needs the same TLC as your nose. Clean the area thoroughly and gently morning and night. If you have a breakout, apply a pimple cream only to the affected area, not to the surrounding skin, and dab it on lightly with your pinky finger. Make sure your hands are clean; you don't want to irritate the already red, sensitive skin. Drink lots of water, eat fresh fruits and vegetables, and try not to touch the zit!

If you have major pimple problems, see a dermatologist. For more minor issues like blocked pores, scheduling a professional skin cleansing at a salon will give your skin a healthy glow for a special occasion.

Protecting Your Skin

If you have fair, sensitive skin and freckles, you should start wearing a facial moisturizer with UV protection: too much exposure to the sun's ultraviolet rays can cause skin damage and skin cancer. You should wear UV protection, even in the winter. In the summer, you might want to use something stronger, like SPF 15 sunscreen. Freckles are beautiful, but they are a sign that your skin needs extra protection. My advice for anyone with skin that freckles easily and heavily is to cover up and bring hats back into fashion! Stay in the shade if you spend hours by the pool, and use sun protection lotion. If you do this, you will stay fresh as a daisy well into old age, you'll save money on medical bills, and you'll never even consider plastic surgery!

Beautiful Bare
Hands and Feet

Well-groomed hands and feet will give you head-to-toe confidence. Trimming and filing your nails, caring for your cuticles, and keeping your skin soft takes time, but when you want to wear sandals or hold hands with a cute guy, you'll be glad you made the effort.

Don't cut either your fingernails or toenails too short, or you will end up with ingrown nails. The prettiest and safest way to give yourself a manicure is to trim your fingernails to your desired length with nail clippers, and then file your nails into soft ovals with an emery board. The rougher side of the board is best for filing your nails short, and the finer side is best for shaping.

Biting your nails is an ugly habit that's difficult to break. Try applying a product from the pharmacy designed specifically to discourage nail-biting (such as an ointment that tastes awful—that ought to work!). Taking pride in your hands by getting a manicure can also help cut out nail-biting; you won't want to ruin all that hard work!

D.I.Y pedicure

To give yourself neat, pretty toenails, use toenail clippers to cut the nails straight across the top. Then, cut the corners so they're as even with the top as you can make them. Use an emery board to file them smooth. Try to avoid filing back and forth on the nail—if you file in one direction, the edge of the toenail will be smoother. Soak your feet in warm water for a minute or two, and then gently push your cuticles back. Smooth some rich moisturizer on your feet and toes (peppermint lotion feels awesome on tired soles). You can wear clear nail polish for a natural look, or pick a brighter color to give your toes a feminine "kick."

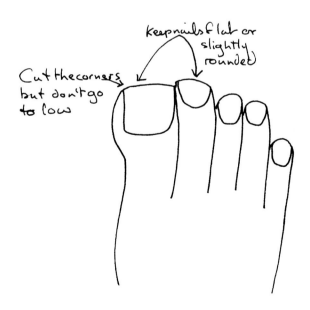

Cut the corners but don't go to low

Keep nails flat or slightly rounded

Hair Removal

I discourage girls from shaving their legs too soon; once you begin removing hair, it seems to grow back longer and thicker, and that makes it hard to go back to not shaving. If you shave your legs, you must do it fairly often—about every two to three days—and you have to deal with stubble.

If you don't like that idea, there are hair removal creams you can use, or you can try waxing. The great thing about waxing your legs is that you don't have to do if very often (only once every one to three months). Go to a salon if you want to try waxing. Doing it yourself is messy and can be painful. Also, try not to wax just before or during your period—your skin is more sensitive then, and the waxing hurts more.

If you have facial hair you want to remove, you should *never* shave it (unless you want stubble—ew!). It's important to think carefully about whether or not you want to start the process of facial hair removal or bleaching. I'd only recommend such a process for girls who have dark, noticeable hair on their upper lip. Most women have facial hair, but on most of us, it's light and not very obvious, and we just live with it. If you want to bleach or remove facial hair, there are many specially designed products that are effective and gentle. Read the instructions carefully before you use any hair removal or bleaching product, especially those intended for the face. Afterward, cleanse your skin as recommended in the product instructions. If the instructions don't mention cleansing, try not to touch your skin for a few hours so you don't irritate it further.

tools and te

Most teens are a bit inexperienced with makeup. You can learn a lot by watching your mom or an older sister apply her makeup in the morning. But even then, you'll probably have a lot of questions about **what** makeup to buy, **how** to put it on, **where** to put it, and **what** tools to use. This section gives you the answers to some of the most common makeup questions, and it also reveals some common teen makeup mistakes. Makeup is about experimenting, but it does take some skill, too. Once you figure out what you need where and how to put it on, you'll be ready to give your mom or your big sister some tips of your own!

Are the right **tools** important?

Clean fingers can be great for applying cream blushes and lip gloss, but not so great for putting on eye makeup or powder blush. Rubbing your fingers on eye shadow powders will cause an oily film (yuck) and make them more difficult to use afterward. You don't need very expensive tools to transform yourself, but there are some important items you should have in your kit that will make things a lot easier. A few applicators and good brushes, a sponge for base application, a cotton powder puff for powder, eye shadow applicators, and cotton swabs for cleaning up any mess are all you really need.

If you already have lots of applicators and/or brushes around, clean them regularly. Wash them with hot soapy water (as hot as you can stand), rinse them thoroughly, dip them in alcohol, and then squeeze them gently into shape (do not rub their heads on a towel as this will deform them). Then let them dry naturally (in sunlight if possible). Clean brushes are even more important if you have blackheads and pimples because dirty brushes will collect and spread oil and dirt.

Create your own personalized travel kit with the brushes and applicators you use most. Cloth brush and makeup holders are great—you can throw them in the wash when they get a little dirty, and you can also personalize them with magic markers and decorations stuck on with fabric glue.

Instead of rushing out and buying a brush set, which often looks good in the store but is not that useful, build up a collection one by one so that you have brushes you can really use. Nice brushes that are firm and have good shape wash well without losing their hair. They will last a long time, and they make applying products easier. Here's a tip for testing a good brush: sweep it across the back of your hand. The head of the brush should spring back into shape easily, but it shouldn't feel rough or irritating on your skin.

Do I need **concealer,** and when should I use a **base?**

If you have a great glow and even skin, you don't have to wear base and concealer every day. Concealer and base are necessary for special occasions when you want a more polished look. Deep-set eyes often have a deeper halo around them. In normal circumstances, this can be very attractive and make the eyes look larger, but when the halo becomes dark and accentuated by lack of sleep, you may want to apply a little concealer to the under-eye area in the inner corners to soften it.

Use your fingertip or a synthetic-haired brush to apply a little concealer where needed (the sketch on the right shows where to dot it). A synthetic brush is best for this because it is flatter and allows a smoother application of the concealer. This kind of brush is also good for dotting concealer on pimples.

Do I have to wear base to hide my **pimples?**

To hide pimples, you may not need base at all— just use a medicated cover-up (concealer) right on the pimple. Dot the product directly on the zit (this is called "spotting"), but not on the area around the pimple—you don't want to dry out the skin. Applying concealer to cover up redness and pimples does not necessarily aggravate your skin condition, and if it helps you avoid touching the blemishes, it can actually make the condition a lot better. Touching your pimples is the worst thing you can do! If you use a medicated or nonmedicated cover-up, it is essential that you wash your face and remove all the product before you go to bed.

The brush above is good for applying concealer under your eyes to get rid of dark circles. The hair is synthetic, so it blends oily or wet products smoothly and stays flat.

How should I apply **base?**

A base is for special occasions. Try it on your inner arm to see if it matches your skin tone before you purchase it. You can put it on with your fingers (make sure they're clean) or use a sponge or a large, flat, synthetic brush like the one on the right. Dampen the sponge before applying your base to get finer coverage.

To apply your base, dot it down the center of your face and blend it lightly outward with your fingertips or the brush.

What is **powder** for, and do I need it?

You only need powder on top of your base if you really want your makeup to stay on well or if you'd like a matte, sophisticated look. You can dust on a compact or loose powder *without* base, too, for a matte finish. If you are wearing base, just make sure the color of the powder is not darker than the color of the base or your skin will look dull and uneven. If you have light skin, choose a translucent powder to give your face a delicate finish. Darker skin will need something more matched to the skin tone. If your skin has yellow undertones, stick with yellow shades of powder. If you need to brighten your skin, go with a peachy-colored powder.

For applying powder, it's nice to have a large, soft, fluffy brush. Everyone should have one—they look and feel great and are also ideal for dusting hair off your face if you have been cutting your bangs.

How do I use **shimmery powder** and **glitter?**

Shimmery powders look gorgeous on bare shoulders and arms and they draw attention to certain parts of your face. They can look great dusted over the entire face, too, but unless you have perfect, clear skin, you should avoid wearing too much shine and just dust or blend cream shimmer over your cheekbones.

Stronger gold or bronze shimmer is best for deeper skin tones. Opalescent shimmer (lighter ones that glow and sparkle), paler golds, and pearls look beautiful on both dark and light skins. Silver and gold will make you look like a goddess at a special party. To apply them quickly and make them stronger, apply them with a wet brush.

Before you apply a shimmery shadow or cream, test it on your arm first—see how strong the shimmer effect is so you don't overdo it. Glitter is the same—save it for the parts of your face you want to draw attention to, like your cheekbones or brows, or just use it in one or two spots for decoration like we did on Sweet Katrina (p. 70).

How should I apply **blush?**

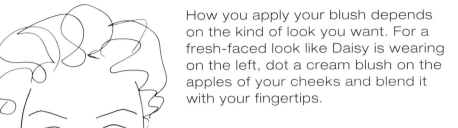

How you apply your blush depends on the kind of look you want. For a fresh-faced look like Daisy is wearing on the left, dot a cream blush on the apples of your cheeks and blend it with your fingertips.

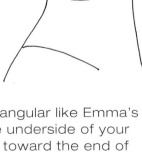

For more sophistication and to heighten your cheekbones the way we did for Liz's look above, you should apply your blush on the cheekbone and blend it toward the nose.

To make your face look more angular like Emma's above, apply your blush to the underside of your cheekbone and blend it down toward the end of your nose.

It's easy to blend creams and tints onto clean skin with your fingertips; their consistency looks fresh and adds to your natural glow.

How do I pluck my eyebrows?

All you need to do is just "clean" up your eyebrows, you don't want to go overboard. The more you pluck, the more maintenance your brows will need. To make your brows look nicely groomed and shaped, here's what you do: pluck the hair between your brows as well as the hair under the outer corner of the brows. Always disinfect your tweezers before you use them by dipping them in rubbing alcohol.

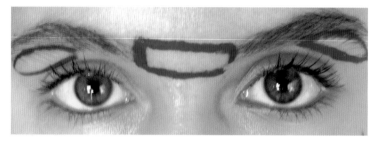

    I don't recommend plucking above your brows; that makes them look very artificial. If you want to wax your brows, make sure you are totally sure about the shape you want. You don't want super-arched brows that make you look like you're always surprised! The good thing about plucking is that you do it one hair at a time; if you decide you want your brows thinner or more shaped, you can go back in under the brows and pluck where you want the arch to be. When you pluck, add shape little by little so you are less likely to make a dramatic mistake!

Stretch the skin around the hairs with one hand. In your other hand, hold the tweezers and slip the point under the hair. Grasp the hair firmly and pull it out in the direction in which it grows (upward and outward).

What do I use to apply **eye shadow?**

Sponge-tipped applicators work very well. Once you have used a sponge-tip for one color, use a fresh one to apply a new color or the makeup will come out looking muddy. Try using just one side of the applicator for one color and the other side for another. Sponge-tips are really good for loose pearlized shadows because they hold the powder well, and then you can press it onto your eyelid before you blend it. Use the point of the applicator to apply eye shadow in the inner corner of your eyelid or to line the lids with shadow.

    A small firm brush like the blue one above is great for small areas of the eyelid—for instance, at the base of the lashes or in the crease of the eye. It's also good for applying dots of highlighting eye shadow (colors lighter or brighter than the "base" eye shadow) in certain areas. Use a larger brush (like the peach-colored one in the photo) to cover the entire eyelid area with shadow—a light color will make your eyes look brighter, and a deep shadow will make your eyes look more dramatic.

about EYE SHADOW

Deep matte shades of eye shadow have no shine; they make your eyes look deeper. Iridescent shadows lighten and brighten your lids. The darker iridescent shades can also deepen your eyes if you wear them around the eyes with a lighter-colored shadow on the brow bone. Wearing a lighter shadow in the inner corners of your eyes will make them look farther apart, which is good if you have a narrow face.

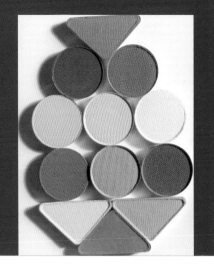

Should I use pencil, powder, or liquid eyeliner?

If you want a soft effect, use a powder. If you want to give your eyes more depth, use an eye pencil. You can work the line of color into the base of your lashes and make your eyes stronger, or you can use the liner in the inner rim of the eyes for a really intense look. A liquid or cake liner will make your eyes look more sophisticated.

If you have a heavy but small eyelid (like Skye, our model in the picture below), using liner under *and* inside the eyes can strengthen them. Don't use light colors on your eyelid, though, because that will be distracting.

How do I apply eyeliner?

To apply eyeliner, begin in the outer corner of the eye—it is usually best to keep the line heaviest there. Hold your eyelid closed with the index finger of your opposite hand, and very gently pull the outer corner out so your lid is not wrinkled. Then, draw as thin a line as possible at the very base of your lashes (make the line a bit heavier if your lashes are blonde), going from the outer corner in. The line should be thickest at the outer corner, and it should become thinner as you go above the pupil and toward the inner corner of the eye.

To apply powder liner, use a small eyeliner brush (like the green one in the photo on the left) with a dark shade of powder eye shadow. Dip the tips of the bristles in the powder to make sure they get a good amount of color. Dab the tips of the bristles along your lash line, again going from the outer corner in. Dip the brush again if you run out of color. For a more defined look, wet the bristles slightly and use cake liner rather than powder.

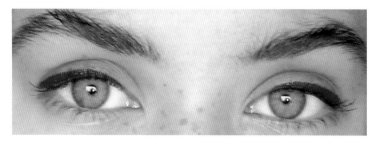

What kind of **mascara** should I use?

A nonwaterproof mascara is gentle enough for everyday wear. Waterproof mascara is great for the beach and weddings or other occasions when you need it to last all day—through outdoor weather or tears of joy. Brown is the most natural-looking mascara for most skin and hair colors (unless you are very dark), but that doesn't mean brown is best. You might want to make your eyes stand out by wearing black mascara, which really makes your lashes "pop," no matter what kind of coloring you have. Black mascara is also a must if you are wearing black eyeliner. Mascara colors such as green and blue are fun, and they can make your eyes look soft and pretty. White mascara looks unique and great if you wear it with a light neutral or white eye shadow; it will also brighten your colored mascaras if you apply it to your lashes first.

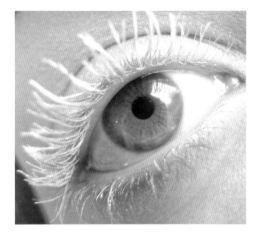

When should I use an **eyelash curler?**

If you choose to use an eyelash curler, do it before you apply your mascara. Open the "jaws" of the curler and position it so that it's a little before the base of your lashes. Gently close the curler and press; hold it there for about a count of five. Then release. Don't forget to open it *before* taking it away from your eye!

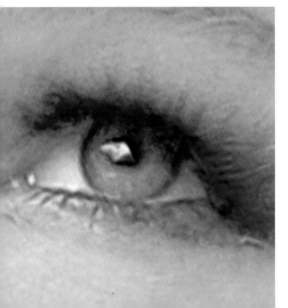

What about **false eyelashes?**

Yes exactly! What *about* false eyelashes? Well, they are lots of fun, come in many colors and shapes, and are easier to remove than glitter. Colored false lashes can turn boring makeup into something special. Finish your eye makeup application and then apply them—it'll be much easier that way. Lightly apply the eyelash glue (it comes with the lashes and is safe—don't use any other kind) to the base of the band of lashes (never, ever directly on your eye!) and let them sit for a few seconds. Then pick them up with tweezers or your fingertips and press them gently into the base of your eyelashes so that the ends are curling up toward your eyebrow. Press until they feel firmly in place.

Turquoise lashes can turn boring makeup into something quite FAB!

How should I apply lip color?

If you want to wear lipstick in a cool, bright shade, use a lip brush to help distribute the color evenly. Apply the lip color first (either with your finger or with the lipstick wand), and then use the lip brush to blend more of the color right to the edge of the lips to make a more voluptuous shape.

Lip glosses and lip stains are easy to wear—just smooth them on using the wand provided or with your finger. Sheer gloss is shiny, soft, and natural-looking. Deep, tinted gloss makes your lips look luscious. Lip stains are a great pick-me-up if you aren't wild about the way gloss makes your lips feel. Stains just give a little more color to the lips, but they're not as heavy as real lipstick. You can also get the look of a lip stain if you just rub your fingertip lightly on some real lipstick and then softly glide it onto your lips.

How do **braces** affect my lip color choice?

Bright lip colors can be lots of fun with braces, but as a rule, it is usually better to play down your lips with a soft gloss or lip color and avoid anything ultra shiny or frosted.

using col

Color is a magical, simple way to **enhance** your features and express your mood. A touch of color on your eyes, lips, or cheeks can jump-start your day, calm you down, or cheer you up. Once you have an understanding of simple color theories (and many of you may already from your art classes), you can organize your makeup colors and **mix and match** them to obtain different effects. You will also be able to **adapt** many of the makeup styles you see in this book to suit your coloring. The world is not black and white, so express yourself **in color**.

or

Mixing Colors

The three **primary** colors—blue, red, and yellow—are pure colors that cannot be made by mixing other colors. That's why they're called primary.

On the left is some makeup in primary colors: red lip color, yellow lip gloss, and blue eye shadow.

The **secondary** colors—orange, green, and violet—can be created by mixing the primary colors. For example:

yellow + blue = green
red + yellow = orange
red + blue = **violet.**

On the right is some makeup in secondary colors: orange lip color, violet blush, and green eye shadow.

By mixing, you can make many, many other shades of the secondary colors. Adding more of one primary color than the other will give the mix a stronger **tint** of the main color (e.g., a little yellow plus a lot of blue equals bluish-green).

Make a **pastel** shadow or lipstick color by starting with a white shadow or lip color, and then adding touches of a different color to the white. If you've ever made frosting for cookies or cakes, you probably played with food coloring to get the frosting pink or green or yellow. It's a similar concept here: you're mixing bright color into a white base to get a lighter shade of the bright color. So, let's say you want to mix a pastel pink lip color—you would start with a white base, then mix in some red until you get the shade of pink you want. If you wanted to make a light pastel blue eye shadow, you'd add dark blue shadow to white shadow.

You can create **muted** shades by adding black to a color. If you want a muted red lip color, mix in some black until the shade is less bright. Here are some more possibilities:

black + yellow = khaki
black + blue = a dusty blue
black + red = a dusty red.

Go slowly when you custom-mix color: it is easy to add more, but if you go too dark, you will have to add more white and things get tricky.

Harmony & Contrast

Warm colors are in the family of yellow, orange, and red. **Cool colors** are in the family of blue, violet, and green. Of course, that is a very simple explanation of a pretty complicated concept—there are many different shades of colors, and some are a lot cooler or a lot warmer than others. Basically, though, when we say a color is warm, we mean it has tones of yellow, orange, or red, and when we say a color is cool, we mean it has tones of violet, blue, or green.

Harmonizing makeup uses either all cool colors or all warm colors.

A **monochromatic** harmony is makeup that uses shades of the same color on all the features, for instance, brown eye shadow, brown blush, and brown lipstick.

You can add an accent to a monochromatic makeup with a touch of a **contrasting** color. That means that you would add an accent of a warm color, like a soft rose, to contrast with a cool color, like lilac. Or you'd add a cool color, like pale emerald, to contrast with with a warm color, like bronze. A contrasting makeup is one that uses a warm color on one part of the face, and a cooler shade of color on another part of the face.

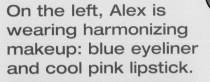

Cool Colors / Warm Colors

On the left, Alex is wearing harmonizing makeup: blue eyeliner and cool pink lipstick.

On the right, Alex is wearing makeup in contrasting colors: warm orange lip color with cool blue eyeliner.

This is Esra wearing makeup in a monochromatic harmony: pink blush, pink lipstick, and pink eye shadow.

Notice how Natalie's lips and eyes stand out in this photo. That is because the warm colors on her eyes contrast with and accentuate the cool colors on her lips.

Inspire Your Inner **Artist**

Use your eyes and imagination to get inspiration for your color mixes. Fashion magazines are a good place to start, but you can also be inspired by art. Look in art books, go to a museum, and pay attention to the combinations of colors you see in paintings. You'll be thrilled at the way Picasso or Monet can inspire you to try different combinations of color on your face.

Here is another way to spark your imagination. I have created a painting in four different color schemes on my computer. I also made a black-and-white print of the painting. Photocopy the black-and-white painting (make several copies) and use makeup colors inspired by the different paintings on p. 39 to color it in. Look at the colors in each painting and see if you can create a "wearable" look using makeup in shades and combinations of those colors. You don't have to limit yourself to the color schemes in the paintings—create some palettes of your own and discover the combinations that appeal to you.

finding the RIGHT SHADES for you

I encourage you to experiment with color—I believe that if you like the way something looks, you should try it. But for those of you who prefer to have guidelines, here are some mistake-proof combinations.

* If you are a redhead, wear eye shadow in a warm brown or green and lip color in warm beige, brick, or coral. Auburn-haired beauties will also look good in violet eye shadow, especially if they have green eyes. (With violet eye makeup, use a softer, more muted pink color on your lips.)

* If you are a fair-skinned blonde, accentuate your fragility with eye shadow in whites and pearls, lilacs, and soft blues and grays; use lip colors in pale pearls or stronger pinks.

* If you are a dark blonde or a light brunette, avoid colors that are too bright and instead go for a smokier look; do your eyes in cool browns and muted shades of blue and green with highlights of shine, and wear muted lip glosses.

* If you are a pale-skinned brunette with blue or dark brown eyes, try violet eye shadow and cool pinks on your lips and cheeks. Charcoal gray and black shadow and liner will give your eyes drama.

* I love using olive eye shadows and gold on olive skin to highlight it naturally, but if you have an outgoing personality and you want something more dramatic, then you should use cooler eye shadow colors such as midnight blue, violet, or pink.

* Very dark skin with a red undertone can't go wrong with bronze and copper eye shadow and lip color; deep black skin looks lovely with silver and blue on the eyelids and cool, muted lip colors.

* Eye shadow in ivory and gold emphasizes the beautiful buff, cream tones of Asian skin naturally.

MAKEUP
TRANSFORMATIONS

Is your personal style **classic**, **cool**, **sweet**, **sporty**, **retro**, **glamorous**, or even **way-out-rageous**? Would you like to be able to change your style to fit your mood? Whether you wake up feeling like a movie star, the next Sofia Coppola, an Olympic athlete, a rock star, or the debate team star, this section is full of makeup tips that will show you how to express all the different things you can be.

clas

A **classic** look is well balanced and polished—great for your graduation day photos, a presentation in front of your class, meeting your new boyfriend's parents, or a visit to a prospective college. **Classic** means elegant, not messy. **Classic** is always in style, never trendy. **Classic** is 100% good taste, not in-your-face. For **classic** makeup,

sic

all the facial features have fairly equal intensity and are

defined very subtly. Its colors are most often harmonious,

and if the eye color is bright, it is applied delicately on the

part of the eyelid right next to the eye. **Classic** makeup

is low key, but wow! You won't have to yell to get noticed—

all you'll have to do is smile.

classic SUZANNE

Suzanne is wearing base and powder. On her eyelids, she is wearing an **opalescent** lilac shadow blended up to the brows. A brown eye shadow powder with a golden undertone is blended under her eyes at the base of the lashes to define and **enlarge** her big blue eyes. I chose this color because it is not distracting, and it **harmonizes** with her golden blonde hair. If you have darker skin and coloring, you may want to substitute a darker shade of brown eye shadow under the eye (not black, though—that would be too harsh). Suzanne is wearing a brown mascara, and her brows have been **defined** with two colors of brow pencil: blonde and taupe.

She is wearing a light, burnt-orange lip color applied with a lip brush for extra precision, and a **matching** shade of blush on her cheeks.

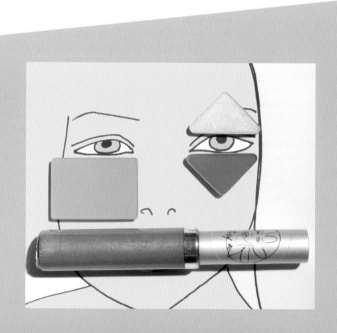

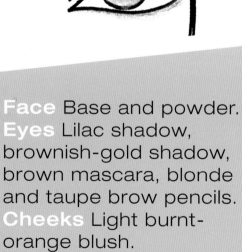

Face Base and powder.
Eyes Lilac shadow, brownish-gold shadow, brown mascara, blonde and taupe brow pencils.
Cheeks Light burnt-orange blush.
Lips Light burnt-orange lip color.

classic KaTRINa

This is standard, **classic** makeup: the darker shade of eye shadow is applied to just past the crease of the eyelid, the lighter shade is applied under the brows. Katrina's lip color **matches** the color of her blouse, which is another **classic** detail.

Katrina has base, concealer, and powder on her skin.

Her eyes are shaded lightly with a **soft** brown on the lids and are highlighted under the eyebrow with a **delicate** ivory highlighting shadow. A little brown shadow is blended under the eye in the outer corner, and the upper lashes are lined with a **fine** line of dark brown eye pencil.

She's wearing black mascara and a **soft** pink lipstick.

Her cheeks are **highlighted** with a **matching** powder blush applied from the top of the cheekbones down toward the apples of the cheeks. The lip, cheek, and blouse colors all match, but because the makeup colors were used delicately, they aren't overpowering.

Face Base, concealer, and powder.
Eyes Soft brown shadow, ivory highlighting shadow, dark brown eyeliner, black mascara.
Cheeks Soft pink blush.
Lips Soft pink lipstick to match blush.

classic DaISY

If you have blue eyes that seem to change color depending on what you wear, this eye makeup will make them appear greener. It will also brighten dark eyes. Wear the same colors shown here on Daisy, or choose a **color that matches** the shade of your eyes. Many people have a touch of another color (or colors) in their eyes—look closely, and use the color that you see. It may be gold, russet, or green.

Daisy is wearing a **lightweight** beige base with a little powder and a touch of warm cream blush.

We applied a dusting of **soft** turquoise shadow up to and in the crease of Daisy's eyelids, and we lined her eyes with a blue pencil liner at the very base of the upper lashes. The liner is applied more thinly in the inner corners of the eyes and more thickly in the outer corners to **emphasize** her almond-shaped eyes. Her black mascara is applied very lightly.

She is wearing a **soft** pink lip gloss on her lips.

Face Lightweight base, a touch of powder.
Eyes Soft turquoise shadow, blue pencil eyeliner, black mascara.
Cheeks Warm cream blush.
Lips Soft pink gloss.

classic Jessica

My student Nikki started Jessica's makeup by applying a base as near as possible to Jessica's **natural** skin tone to even it out.

Then she applied a little warm orange-red cream blush on the apples of her cheeks to give them a natural **glow**.

Jessica's eyes are lined with a black pencil liner applied to the inner rim of the eyelid. A dark brown shadow was blended over her eyelids, and then we highlighted them in the center with a taupe shadow that has a soft **shimmer**.

We gently applied a touch of **warm** russet blush (the same color we used on Daisy) to the outer corners of Jessica's eyes, under the brow.

On her lips, Jessica is wearing a **soft** brown shade of gloss.

Face Base.
Eyes Black pencil eyeliner, dark brown shadow, taupe shimmer, warm orange-red blush.
Cheeks Warm, orange-red cream blush.
Lips Soft brown gloss.

classic SARAH

S arah is wearing a liquid base, **soft** tawny (sandy light brown) cream blush, and powder. Her brows have been brushed to clean the powder from them.

An apricot eye shadow was blended from the base of the eyes next to the lashes up to the brows. For those of you with no red in your hair, replace the apricot with a taupe shadow. A little dark brown eye shadow powder in the outer third of the eye was blended upwards—no further than the crease—to **open** the eyes. We used brown mascara to give the eyes a finishing touch and **strengthen** Sarah's blonde lashes.

We applied a gloss to her lips, and then we **emphasized** their beautiful shape by **defining** them **lightly** with a brick lip color.

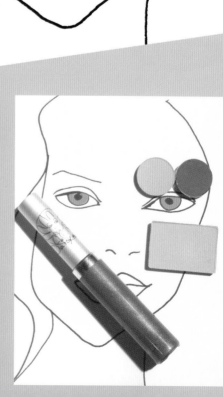

Face Liquid base, powder.
Eyes Apricot eye shadow, dark brown eye shadow, brown mascara.
Cheeks Soft, sandy, light brown cream blush.
Lips Brick lip color.

classic TaNIa

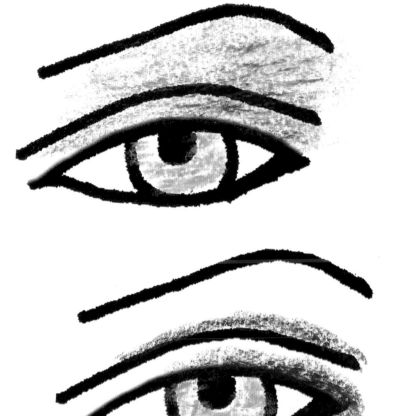

Tania's makeup is a warm **harmony** of soft red-browns.

A little concealer was applied under her eyes, and we used a tawny blush on her cheeks.

On her eyes, a **soft** red-brown eye shadow was applied to the base of her lashes, tapering off to her brows to give a natural **glow** to her eyelids. The crease of her eyelid was deepened with a touch of a deeper brown shadow, which was also used to **define** the lashes **lightly** in the outer, upper, and lower corners of the eyes. The lighter shadow is applied from the lids to the brow; the darker shade is applied in the crease and in the upper and lower outer corners of the eye.

A **warm** coral-pink gloss was used on her lips.

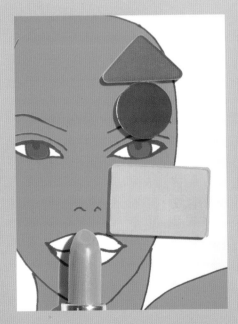

Face Concealer.
Eyes Soft red-brown eye shadow, deeper brown eye shadow.
Cheeks Tawny powder blush.
Lips Coral-pink gloss.

cool

Being cool means being confident and secure about yourself. Cool is noticeable, not ordinary. It's bold, not boring. It's unique, not copycat. You can have cool makeup by using just one special product with lots of attitude. You can wear a cool look any day or for any occasion if you want to attract attention. Cool makeup is most often very simple—you don't need base, concealer, or powder. A beautiful metallic silver eye shadow in either cream or powder

will do the trick: blend it from the base of your upper eyelashes

right up to your eyebrows in one large swoop. A bright color

on the eyes alone is **cool**, or you can wear it with an unusual

color of lip gloss or lipstick in a contrasting color. Check

out the photos of the girls in this section and get inpired

to explore the Gwen Stefani or Avril LaVigne in you!

cool SUZANNE

A little **color** dotted above and below the pupils of the eyes is a quick and effective way to **accentuate** them and look **cool**. Try violet or green for green eyes, yellow for amber ones, and blue or violet for brown eyes. Wear the eye makeup by itself, or add it to a more classic makeup to give the look a little **edge**. If you use a cream eye color, press a little glitter into it to attract more **attention**.

Suzanne is wearing base and powder, her brows are lightly defined, and she is wearing a brown lipstick.

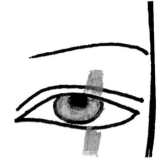

Face Base and powder.
Eyes Blue shadow above and green shadow below pupils, light brown brow pencil.
Lips Brown lipstick.

cool KaTRina

Eyes White eyeliner.
Lips Bright red lipstick.

Katrina was used to seeing herself with a more soft, innocent look, and she had never done this type of makeup on herself before (she said she would not have even thought about doing it). We really **transformed** Katrina with some easy, fast steps.

We used **simple** white eyeliner and **bright** red lipstick. If you try this, make sure you use the red color to just **tint** your lips; don't coat them heavily with the lipstick. If you do that, the look will be way too strong and off balance, and the color will smudge on the edges of your lips and maybe even your teeth (and that would NOT be **cool**).

cool **Daisy**

Thus **cool** look is one of Daisy's favorites. This eye shadow looks white but when you put it on, it is **iridescent** lilac. Just blend it over the entire eyelid with an eye shadow brush to make your eyes **shine**. Lightly outline your lips as we did Daisy's with soft pink lip pencil, and top off the look with a white **pearly** lip color to create some irresistible **drama**.

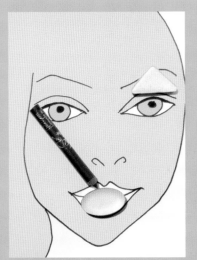

Eyes Iridescent lilac shadow. **Lips** Soft pink lip liner, white pearly lip color.

cool JENNIFER

Jennifer is wearing a base to **even** out her skin tone. Blue is **cool** in more ways than one, especially when it's worn with a warm colored blush that's unusually placed. We applied a **dark** blue eye shadow more **intensly** at the base of her lashes and blended it outward. She's wearing blue mascara.

We applied warm blush slightly under her cheekbone and blended it downward to **slim** Jennifer's face.

To add some contrast to her blue eye makeup, we applied lots of black **tinted** gloss to her lips.

Face Base.
Eyes Dark blue eye shadow, blue mascara.
Cheeks Warm blush.
Lips Black tinted gloss.

cool SaRaH

A simple yet special **contrasting** color combination—like the green eye shadow and orange lip **color** Sarah is wearing—can be very cool and **unexpected**. Violet eye color with orange would ring some bells, too.

Because she had a slight tan, we applied a **pale** lightweight liquid base and a light dusting of translucent powder on Sarah. Pale skin brings out the color in your eyes, lips, and hair if you're a redhead.

We blended a warm-colored blush over the apples of Sarah's cheeks.

To make the **strong** green cream eye shadow more wearable, keep it on the part of the lid close to the lashes.

We **lightly** applied **bright** orange lipstick to Sarah's lips.

Face Lightweight base, translucent powder.
Eyes Green eye shadow.
Cheeks Warm blush.
Lips Bright orange lipstick.

cool TANIA

Tania is wearing a warm shade of base that closely matches her skin tone, along with a light powder to even out her coloring. The two **extremes—heavy** dark khaki-green eye makeup together with **very pale** lips—make for an extremely cool look with plenty of **attitude**.

We used lots of khaki powder eye shadow around Tania's eyes at the base of the lashes and in the crease of her eyes. We chose to use a creamy navy pencil eyeliner at the base of her upper lashes, and we extended the line a little and gave her eyes some extra sizzle with lots of black mascara.

For her lips, we went way-pale to make a **striking** contrast with her way-dark eyes. We chose a **nude** lip color of the same intensity as Tania's base color (without lip liner), to complete this look.

Face Base and light powder.
Eyes Dark, khaki-green eye shadow, navy pencil eyeliner, black mascara.
Lips Nude lip color.

swe

Sweet is delicate and fresh, not overwhelming. **Sweet** is romantic and feminine, with a balance of colors. For a sweet look, make your brown eyes look round and innocent, but then go easy on the mouth—you don't want strong eyes *and* strong lips for this look. The strong smoky eye with no lip color at all is **sweet** as honey on a round face, but it would be too strong on a more

et

angular face. On an angular face, the eye makeup should be soft. A light pink harmony looks great with any coloring, and what could be sweeter than the color of cotton candy? If you are a gentle soul, this look is a great choice. For those of you who want to capture the attention of someone shy, a **sweet** look will do the trick; wear it to a party and see if your sweetie can resist!

sweetSUZaNNe

Eyes Lime-green shadow, mediterranean blue-green shadow.
Cheeks Soft peachy/corn-colored blush.
Lips Transparent gloss.

To keep her makeup **delicate** and balanced, Suzanne's strong eye color is **sweetened** with a soft **transparent** lip gloss.

An acid lime-green is blended around her eyes very delicately, making her **innocent** blue eyes look greener. A slightly deeper shade of mediterranean blue-green is blended around Suzanne's eyes at the base of the lashes.

We blended a **soft** peachy/corn shade of blush over her cheeks.

sweetDAISY

D aisy has a **rounded** face, so she is able to do a strong **smoky** eye and still look soft, as long as she keeps her lips and cheeks very **soft** also.

Matte shades of brown, gray, and a touch of black shadow were used around her eyes, but we blended them well to maintain softness without harsh lines. Apply the gray shadow over the eyelid and under the eye. Apply the brown in the inner corner and into the outer corner over the gray. Blend the black *into the gray* around the eyes at the base of the lashes, keeping it very close to the lashes, strengthening it in the outer corner in the crease of the eye.

Apply lots of black mascara, but if you are blonde, use brown mascara.

Daisy is wearing no base or powders— just a little concealer and a **transparent** lip gloss that doesn't "fight" with her strong eye makeup.

Face A little concealer.
Eyes Matte gray eye shadow, matte brown eye shadow, black eye shadow, black mascara (blondes should use brown mascara).
Lips Transparent lip gloss.

sweet KaTRina

Here's a look that's both sweet and unusual. It's all about **balance**—you don't want strong color on all of your features. So here, no base or powder was applied to Katrina's skin, just a little concealer and a soft pink cream blush.

A light **shimmery** pink shadow was blended from the base of her upper lashes to the brow, and the area under her eyes and close to the upper lashes was emphasized with a deeper pink-brown shadow.

Katrina's wearing a soft **icy** pink lip gloss.

To attach **glitter** and hearts, we applied a dot of turquoise cream shadow to the outer corner of Katrina's eyes and a **transparent** gloss to one cheekbone. Then we pressed the glitter into those products. For jewels, you will need flat-backed fake stones and some eyelash glue. Put the dot of eyelash glue on the part of your face where you would like to apply the jewel, and wait a few seconds until it becomes sticky to the touch. Then press the stone onto the glue and hold it there for a few seconds until the glue dries.

Face A little concealer, glitter (held in place with a dot of cream shadow and transparent gloss), and fake jewels (applied with eyelash glue).
Eyes Light, shimmery pink shadow, deeper pink-brown shadow.
Lips Soft icy-pink gloss.

sweet SARAH

You don't have to wear pink to look sweet. As you can see on Sarah in this photo, **bright** colors can be just as **fresh** and charming if you use them right! Sarah is wearing base and powder to even out her skin tone and soften her freckles.

A dark blue pencil dotted into the very base of her upper and lower lashes **accentuates** and enlarges her eyes because of the contrasting colors. Dotting pencil liner under the eyes makes look them more clear and **serene**, and brown mascara softly **defines** them. We made Sarah's eyes look even softer by applying a light, shimmery shadow with a **hint** of lilac over the rest of the eyelid.

Her lips are defined with a ruby lip color. If you're using a stong lip color with a sweet look, make sure that you apply it slightly within your natural lip line and that you don't use the color too heavily.

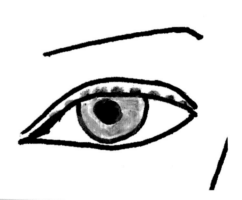

Face Base and powder.
Eyes Soft shimmery light lilac shadow, dark blue eye pencil, brown mascara.
Lips Ruby lipstick.

sweetLUCINDa

Soft violets and lilacs look great on blondes, and they are subtle enough for a **sweet** look. They look sort of **hazy** and pretty.

Lucinda is wearing a base and a warm cheek color to blend in with her skin tone. This allows her **cooler** shaded eyes and lips to be more noticeable.

What could have become really glamorous makeup is kept sweet by using **gentle** blush placement and lip gloss instead of a strong lip color.

We blended an **iridescent** lilac shadow over her eyelids and above and under her eyes in the inner corners. Violet accentuates green eyes, so we blended a deep shade of violet shadow in the creases of her lids, and we also applied it below the outer corner of the eye and blended it outward. We applied violet cake eyeliner, which is mixed with water, to the very base of the lashes; the line is a little thicker in the outer, upper corner of the eye.

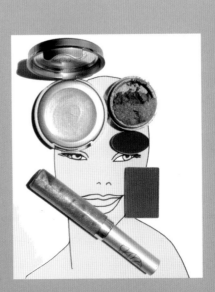

Face Base.
Eyes Iridescent lilac shadow, deeper violet shadow, violet cake eyeliner.
Cheeks Warm blush.
Lips Lip gloss.

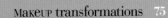

sweet Tania

There is more than one shade of pink! Give slightly brown skin a juicy boost by using this **pure** shade. We're not talking about hot pink here—that's a little too wild for a sweet **fairytale** look. We started with the same way-out-rageous pink you see Tania wearing on p.117, but we softened it and blended it to create a look that's pure **princess**.

Tania is matching concealer, base, and powder.

We **blended** violet eye shadow over a light layer of pink eye shadow and eyeliner, then softened the colors by rubbing them lightly with a dry cotton swab. We then applied a soft taupe shadow on top to mute them a bit more.

A lighter lip is a necessity for a sweeter look, especially when you have a more angular face or want to wear a stronger eye makeup. Here Tania is wearing a soft, cool, **frosted** pink lipstick to balance the stronger pink in her eye makeup. To make the lip color more frosty, blend in a little white.

Eyes Taupe shadow (to soften strong pink liner and pink and violet shadow shown on p.117).
Lips Cool, frosted pink lipstick.

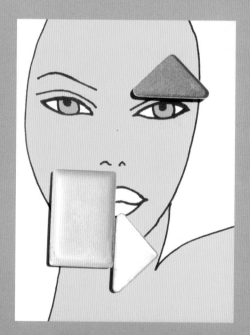

spor

A **sporty** look brings out your clean, healthy, natural radiance, and the makeup is usually not very noticeable. When you're thinking about trying a **sporty** look, you should also think which sport suits you. If you are a figure skater like Lucinda, you may wear more makeup than a soccer player like Sarah. A lifeguard like Tania must think

first and foremost about protecting her skin from too

much sun, but also about accentuating a warm glow. A

sporty look is radiant and effortless; it brings out your

rosy cheeks and a sparkle in your eyes—no matter what

sport appeals to you. You'll make people want to get

up, get outside, and get active!

sporty SUZaNNe

Suzanne loves the **beach** and the sea—she'd like to look like she surfs every day. In this photo, she had just come back from **spring break** in Aruba. She had worn a heavy protection sunscreen, so she only had a hint of a tan.

We strengthened her **tan** look with a much darker, warmer base than she would normally wear and a warm cream blush applied to the center of her cheeks—just where the **sun** might have caught her if she had really been surfing.

To give shine to her lids, we blended a very very pale green cream shadow over them. We used brown mascara for her lashes (more natural looking on a **blonde** than black mascara).

She looked great with nude lip gloss, but we also tried a bright orange to accentuate her smile and fun personality. Hang ten! Suzanne the New Yorker looks just like a Malibu **surfer girl**.

Face Dark, warm base.
Eyes Pale green cream shadow, brown mascara.
Cheeks Warm-colored cream blush.
Lips Bright orange lip gloss.

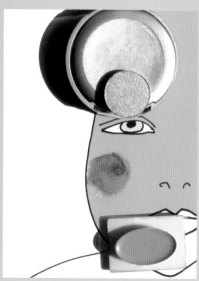

sporty KaTRINa

Most **tennis** players wear a little makeup, so this is a crisp, **perky** look that's perfect for volleying some balls in the **fresh** air of the courts.

Katrina's perfect skin is free of base, and we have applied just a little concealer and powder.

We emphasized her eyes with a pearl shadow on the lid and used a brown shadow under the eyes at the base of the lower lashes and in the outer corners.

She is wearing a nude lip color with gloss on her lips, which are lightly defined with a brown lip pencil. **Score: forty love**. Watch out Wimbledon, here comes Katrina!

Face A little concealer and powder.
Eyes Pearl shadow, brown shadow.
Lips Nude lip color, clear gloss, brown lip pencil.

sporty Daisy

Daisy is an avid **swimmer**—she likes to get a golden tan and she is proud of her **freckles**. The most important product she can put on her face is 30 SPF waterproof sunscreen whenever she's in the **pool** or the **sea**. As much as Daisy prides herself on her freckles, the facial area is one of the most sensitive, and SPF should be reapplied constantly throughout the day. If you have freckles that become darker and larger during the **summertime**, that's a sign of skin damage, and you should be more careful about applying sunscreen regularly. So Daisy's sporty look is as **simple** as it gets: **water** adds a natural shine and sparkle to her hair and skin, and her sunscreen keeps her healthy and **radiant** looking—add an iced tea and a plastic raft, and what more could a girl want?

sporty SARAH

Face A little concealer, sunblock.
Eyes Brown mascara.
Cheeks Light blush, stripes of thick, cream sunblock mixed with blue face paint.
Lips Lip gloss.

Sarah is a **soccer** player, but she still likes to look good on the **playing field**. Wearing makeup for important matches gives her that final burst of **confidence** that motivates her to win the game.

Sarah is wearing a little concealer and a little blush, lip gloss, mascara, and most importantly, sunblock. Sarah asked for makeup that would make her look **intimidating** on the field, so we used stripes of sunblock mixed with blue face paint at the top of her cheekbones. They give her extra protection for her very sensitive skin, and they also make her look like a warrior. Beware goalie—Sarah is cute, but **fierce**!

sporty LUCINDa

L ucinda is a champion **figure skater**.
Even on days when she is training but not
performing, she still needs to look a little
glamorous and protect her skin from the **cold**
with base and powder. Here, she is wearing a
light blue eye shadow, lots of black mascara,
a little blush on the cheekbone, and lots of her
favorite product—lip gloss. (We used an iridescent
one over a tinted black one; the two together
make her lips look soft and pink.) Now she's ready
to hit the **rink** and do some triple axels to her
favorite song.

Face Base, powder.
Eyes Light blue eye
shadow, black mascara.
Cheeks A touch of blush.
Lips Tinted black gloss,
iridescent gloss.

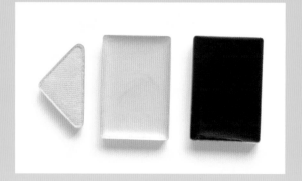

sporty TaNIa

Tania is a **lifeguard** during the summer. Fortunately, she has pretty sturdy skin. Saving lives is a tough job, but when you spend so much time in the **sun**, the threats of skin damage are also very serious. To take care of her skin's health, she protects herself with an oily waterproof sunscreen all the time; this also gives a **glow** to her skin, which she enhances by using a berry-colored cream blush. A **golden**, sparkly cream eye shadow and a yellow lip gloss also help her to maintain a bright **dewy** look, even when she is not in the water. Tania will have all the cute boys at the pool wanting her to come rescue them!

Face Oily, waterproof sunscreen.
Eyes Golden sparkly cream eye shadow.
Cheeks Berry-colored cream blush.
Lips Yellow lip gloss.

Anyone can take a **retro** influence and make it thei

You don't have to end up looking like you just

walked out of a history book or an old movie. Think

of Marilyn Monroe in the '50s, Madonna in the '80

and the actresses who are hot right now. **Retro**

red lips and dark eyeliner are a recurrent theme. Fa

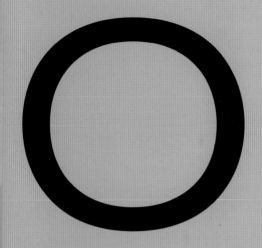 eyelashes on both the upper and lower lashes are obviously **retro** '60s-inspired, and the long shimmery eyes from the '70s disco scene are definitely exciting. Go **retro** and make a look from yesterday a little bit now, a little bit new—but all you! Have fun and turn some heads!

retro Sarah

Sarah has a very **1920s movie-star** feel about her—it's a **dramatic** look, but her makeup is still very wearable and not too over-the-top. Here, her pale, clear skin is bare; she's not wearing any base or powder.

We made her eyes **smokier** (for extra **diva** power) by using liner and shadow with the same red and amber tones as her hair.

We made her lips look very defined (think **Hollywood**) by using a brown lip color mixed with brick red.

To get this look, the eye shadow colors you use must be very matte (not shiny or glittery or pearly). We blended a camel color around Sarah's eyes, and then deepened it with a red-brown color at the base of her lashes. Her eyelashes are accentuated with brown mascara and **feathery, natural, false eyelashes.** If you have darker coloring than Sarah, you should use **black** lashes instead. Wear this look if you feel like a **femme fatale**—just don't break too many hearts!

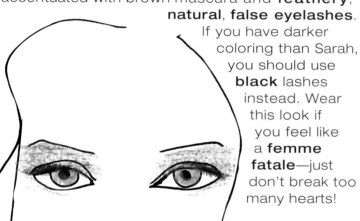

Eyes Matte camel-brown shadow, red-brown shadow, brown mascara, false eyelashes.
Lips Brown lip color mixed with brick red.

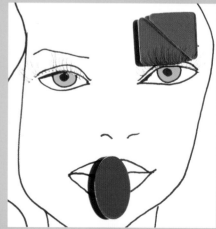

retro Katrina

Another absolutely classic look from the **roaring '20s**. On Katrina, we did a look inspired by Clara Bow, a 1920s actress famous for her **big eyes** and red, **Cupid's-bow** lips. This is the look many **flappers** and actresses from the silent-film era were famous for—it is totally captivating, **mysterious**, and full of high drama.

First, we applied a pale base to even out and lighten Katrina's skin and to help create the **doll-like look** that was so popular in that time period.

Circles of eye shadow under and over the eyes, going up to the lid, make Katrina's eyes look round and **innocent**. You can do this by first blending a soft matte green shadow around the eyes, and then applying a stronger, brighter shade of green to the base of the lashes.

To make your lips look like Katrina's, draw them with lip liner—make the outline small and **bow-like** by staying **inside** your natural lip line, especially at the outer edges. We used matte lipstick (not shiny), and applied white pencil to the cupid's bow (the little *v* in the upper lip) to give it a distinct shape. All you need now is a cool **vintage** dress and you'll look like you just stepped out of *The Great Gatsby!*

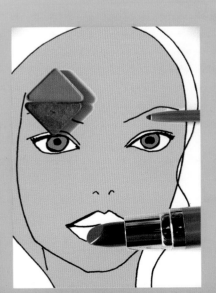

Face Base.
Eyes Soft matte green shadow, bright green shadow
Lips Lip liner, matte lipstick, white lip pencil.

retro Tania

In the **1940s**, the style for makeup was more **fresh-faced** than it was in the '30s or the '50s, and women liked their **eyebrows** to look thicker and more natural. **Red lips** were all the rage. It was easy to transform Tania's sporty look into a retro '40s one. Here's how we did it.

All we needed to do was **glamorize** Tania a bit with touches of color on her eyelids. Copper shine at the base of the lashes added glimmer. We blended a transparent red under the brows for **drama** and a touch of turquoise in the outer corners of her eyes to give more punch.

A soft red **accentuates** her lips, and with a touch of berry-colored blush on her cheeks, we turned what would otherwise be a conventional, monochromatic look into something more unusual. Tania looks like she's getting ready to sing on the stage in a '40s **jazz** club—all she needs is one of those big, old-fashioned microphones.

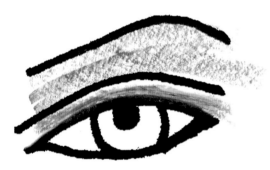

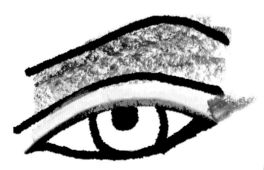

Eyes Copper shine transparent red shadow, turquoise shadow.
Cheeks Berry blush.
Lips Soft red lipstick.

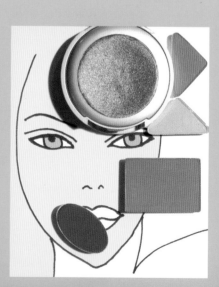

retro suzanne

In the '50s, **rock and roll** and **cool cars** were in, and teenagers were in heaven. Girls wore black **liquid eyeliner** and **bright lipstick**. This look is a total '50s **classic**, and if it is done correctly, it will make anyone look fabulous. To keep it fresh and modern, don't overdo the base, or wear none at all if you have great skin. Here's how you can create this look yourself.

Apply blush in a very soft color (like light pink) to give your face a natural glow—don't use too much.

Keep the eyelids light—either go with no shadow at all, or just use soft shimmer with little or no color. Use **black** liquid eyeliner, and draw the line very close to the upper lashes, extending it only slightly beyond the outer end of your lash line. You could also do this with liquid eyeliner in a different color for a **modern twist**. You can wear a little mascara on the lower lashes and define the upper lashes with a slight dotting of a light brown pencil along the lash line, but this must be very light. The **brows** should be lightly defined in an **arched** shape. Choosing the **right red** lipstick is important. As a loose rule, a red with a slightly orange glow is softer for blondes and redheads; brunettes and girls with darker skin will find it more **striking** to wear reds with a blue undertone. Once you've got your black eyeliner and red lipstick on, throw on a fuzzy sweater and get your dad to take you for a ride in his convertible!

Face Light base.
Eyes Soft shimmer shadow (or none at all), black liquid eyeliner, mascara on lower lashes.
Cheeks Light pink blush.
Lips Red lipstick with a slight orange glow for blondes and redheads; red lipstick with a blue undertone for brunettes and girls with dark skin.

retroLUCINDa

The '60s were full of wild, **bright** colors (think **tie-dye**) and **funky** fashions (think bell-bottoms and mini-skirts) that are also very **hip** today. Lucinda usually lengthens her eyes with shadow or liner, so I felt that this '60s look with the **false eyelashes** and **colorful** shadow blended around the eyes would be a good **change** for her.

First, I used a warm base on her skin, and accentuated her cheeks with a **bronze-**colored blush.

For the eye makeup, place a turquoise shadow very heavily around the eyes at the base of the lashes, then blend it outwards until you have a smooth edge. Dust a translucent **powder** on top of this, then apply a little white eye shadow powder over the turquoise at the base of the upper lashes and in the inner corners of the eye. Apply lots of **mascara** to your own lashes, and then apply false upper and lower eyelashes (see p. 32 for instructions). Totally **psychedelic**, Lucinda—Lenny Kravitz would be proud!

Face Warm base.
Eyes Turquoise shadow, translucent powder, white powder shadow, black mascara, false eyelashes.

retro Daisy

The '70s were the **disco** era: cheeks were accentuated, noses were slimmed with contouring powder, eyes were extended with **lots of shimmer**. The makeup was great for **parties**.

For this look, apply a lot of violet cream shadow around the eye at the base of the lashes. Blend the shadow outward to **lengthen** the eye. Use black pencil inside the lower rim of the lashes and at the base of the upper lashes over the shadow. Sweep translucent face powder over the eyelid, then apply shimmery pink-violet shadow over the eyelid up to the brow, **extending** the shadow outward to the temples. Apply black mascara.

To make your nose look **slimmer**, take a small, clean, eye shadow brush and dip it in brown shadow powder. Dot the powder at the beginning of the brow line, and then blend it lightly down either side of the center of the nose.

Blend a violet-pink blush from the earlobe down toward the mouth, placing it slightly under the cheekbone. **Accentuate** the upper cheekbone with a white powder. Finish with a fuchsia lip color. When you show up at the disco party, there'll be no parking on the **dance** floor!

Nose Brown shadow for contouring.
Eyes Violet cream eye shadow, black pencil liner, translucent powder, shimmery pink or violet shadow, black mascara.
Cheeks Violet-pink blush, white powder.
Lips Fuchsia lip color.

glamo

A **glamorous** look is the greatest pick-me-up. It can do wonders for your morale. Can't find the right shoes for your prom? Just take some extra time on the details of your makeup, and no one will *ever* notice your shoes. Wouldn't you prefer to have everybody looking at your face than your feet? Go for **glammy** shimmer and shine on the eyelids, cheeks, and lips. Make your

rous

lips poutier, your lids shinier, and your eyes larger. Everything can be slightly exaggerated when you're **glamorous**. The cheeks can be sculpted and high-lighted, or you can use a strong lip color. Individual false eyelashes are another way to go **glam**. This is the type of look you will want for your prom, school dances, or fun parties.

glam SUZANNE

Suzanne looks ready for the **runway**! Here, she is wearing base and powder. Her cheeks have been **sculpted** with a soft brown blush applied under the cheekbone and some soft **shine** high on the cheekbone. The deeper matte shade of blush slims down the face, and the **shimmer** accentuates the area where you apply it.

On her lids, Suzanne is wearing a **gold** cream shadow tapering off from the base of the lashes to the brows. Over this, we blended a shimmery **bronze** powder from the base of the lashes toward the outer corners of her eyes, and then we added a little under the eyes. We applied a brown cake eyeliner with a wet brush to the base of the upper lashes and a touch of **silver** shadow to both the upper and lower inner corners of the eyes. We used lots of black mascara on her upper and lower lashes.

For the finishing touch, we applied a soft pink lip color and then blended a much deeper shade of pink over it.

Face Base and powder.
Eyes Gold cream shadow, shimmery bronze powder, brown cake eyeliner, black mascara.
Cheeks Soft brown blush, soft shine.
Lips Soft pink lip color blended with deeper pink.

glam katrina

The true **glamour** in this makeup is the **sparkling**, **polished** feel it has all together. You don't have to wear tons of makeup to pull off this look; sometimes the **right colors** in the **right places** make a big difference.

I used a base and a powder on Katrina's skin for a **glamorous**, smooth finish.

I applied lots of dark brown and black shadow around Katrina's eyes, with a white shade under her brows to give more depth to her eye area (see the top sketch). Her eyes are lined with black at the base of the upper lashes for extra **emphasis** (see the bottom sketch).

Katrina is wearing coral blush blended low over her cheekbones and a soft pink lipstick on her lips.

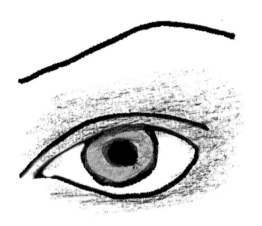

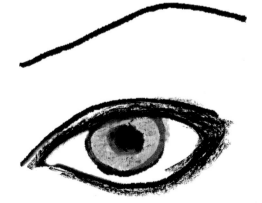

Face Base and powder.
Eyes Dark brown shadow, black shadow, white shadow, black liner.
Cheeks Coral blush.
Lips Soft pink lipstick.

glam Jessica

It wasn't hard to make Jessica feel **glammy**—she is such a fun, **vivacious** person, all I had to do was add a few makeup details to express her inner **spirit** on the outside.

To even out Jessica's skin tone, we applied a base and powder.

To accentuate Jessica's **outgoing** personality, we used bright colors on her eyes. We chose an iridescent green shadow for the lid and crease, and a bronze shadow for under the brow. Jessica's eyes are lined with a black pencil, outside and inside the eye.

We smoothed a warm blush shade on Jessica's cheeks.

We applied a soft pinky-bronze lipstick just inside Jessica's natural lip line to **balance** her lips with her eyes. If you have large lips like Jessica's and would like to soften them, apply lip color just inside the natural edge of the lips. Do not use a pencil liner.

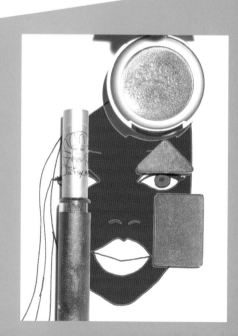

Face Base and powder.
Eyes Iridescent green shadow, bronze shadow, black pencil eyeliner.
Cheeks Warm-colored blush.
Lips Soft pink-bronze lipstick.

glam JENNIFER

Jennifer likes a more **coy**, **playful** look, so we decided to **harmonize** her **snowy** gold eye shadow with her lip color and glamorize those soft colors with false lashes. We used eyebrow pencil to lightly extend both Jennifer and Jessica's eyebrows.

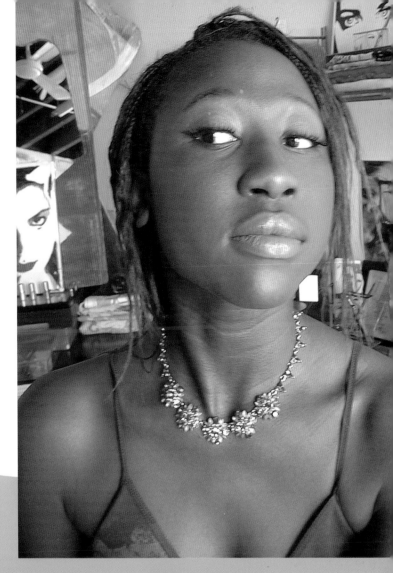

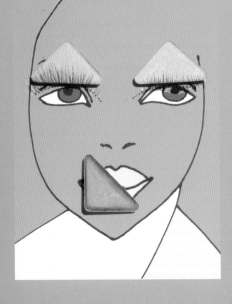

Face Base and powder.
Eyes Snowy gold shadow, false eyelashes.
Cheeks Warm-colored blush.
Lips Snowy gold lip gloss.

glam Sarah

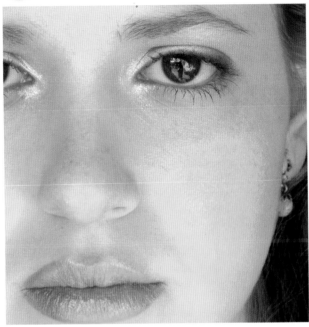

Everyone says redheads should avoid blue and pink, so for this **glamorous** look on Sarah, we thought it would be interesting to break that rule. I think you will agree that she looks **fab** with her pale lips, strong cheeks, and her baby-blue eye makeup.

We started by applying base and powder then applied pale **Carribean**-blue cream eye shadow and strengthened it by applying **seafoam** (another pale blue) powder shadow over it. We used the same blue pencil that we used on Sweet Sarah (p. 72), only this time we just applied it to the base of the upper lashes and inside the lower rim of the eyes. To the inner corner of the eyes, we applied a **shimmery** white **stardust** powder. To complete this glamorous eye, we strengthened the eyebrows with light brown brow pencil.

Lots of strong powder blush was applied to her cheeks and blended downwards. To make her lips **voluptuous**, we applied a soft shimmery pink gloss, then outlined them lightly with a dusty pink pencil. To further accentuate them, we also applied a touch of nude lip color and a white pearly color on top.

Face Base and powder.
Eyes Pale Caribbean-blue cream shadow, seafoam-blue powder shadow, stardust-white powder shadow, blue pencil liner.
Cheeks Strong rosy powder blush.
Lips Soft shimmery pink gloss, nude and pearly white lip colors, dusty pink lip liner.

glam LUCINDA

Lucinda is always **glamorous** on the ice, and she wears the most **stunning** outfits. It is important for her to have a makeup that matches her clothes but that does not make her look too sophisticated, so she always keeps her lips fairly soft with lots of gloss and strengthens her eyes.

Lucinda is wearing a little base and powder.

We blended a smoky gray eye shadow with a shimmery lilac powder over it from the crease of the eyelids to the brows. We dotted a touch of **metallic** turquoise shadow in the inner corners of Lucinda's eyes to **accentuate** their green color, and then applied a black liquid liner to the very base of her lashes, making the line thicker at the outer corners of her eyes and extending it a little beyond the lash line to **elongate** her eyes slightly.

Face Base and powder.
Eyes Smoky gray shadow, metallic turquoise shadow, black liquid eyeliner.
Lips Lots of gloss.

glam Daisy

Daisy asked me to give her a **glamorous** look for her school **graduation** photos. She is wearing a little concealer and some powder.

A burgundy shade of eye shadow was blended around her eyes, softened with a peach and a dusty pink under the brows. I applied lots of black mascara to just the upper lashes and used a soft red lip color with a blue undertone to complete the look.

Daisy's lip and eye makeup were quite **strong**, so I thought it would be better to use a very **natural blush**—three strong points can tend to make your makeup overpowering. Daisy's makeup will make her graduation photos **gorgeous**.

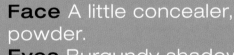

Face A little concealer, powder.
Eyes Burgundy shadow softened with peach and dusty pink shadows. Black mascara.
Cheeks Natural blush.
Lips Soft red lipstick.

glamTANIA

We decided to accentuate the **exotic** side of Tania's personality with this **smoldering** makeup. The end results were so **drop-dead gorgeous,** Tania could have stopped traffic!

We did this by first using a **warm** base with a strong yellow undertone, and then applying an **amber** blush low on her cheekbones.

Lots of black cream shadow with black pencil over it was used around Tania's eyes to make them look deeper and longer. The black pencil was applied inside the upper and lower rim of the eyes. Under the brow on the brow bone, a soft matte **ivory** highlighter gently completes the eye makeup.

Tania's **beautifully shaped** lips were accentuated with a deep-burgundy lip color applied with a lip brush.

Face Warm base with strong yellow undertone.
Eyes Black cream shadow, black pencil liner, soft matte ivory shadow.
Cheeks Amber blush.
Lips Deep burgundy lipstick.

way-out

Everyone feels like being a little wild, a little crazy, and really letting loose sometimes. **Way-out-rageous** makeup is for those times when you feel like you could give Picasso a run for his money. It's for times when you want to experiment with colors, brushes, paints, and powders. It feels great to express yourself in vibrant colors and big brushstrokes! **Way-out-rageous** is pure play—it's a style that looks wicked in a music video— but it's definitely not for school. It could mean wearing

rageous

bright face paint to a concert. It could mean creating

way-out-rageous fashion-model looks when you and

your friends are at home imitating Tyra Banks at a photo-

shoot. Or, **way-out-rageous** could simply mean breaking

out of your routine and wearing blue mascara with black

eyeliner. **Way-out-rageous** is for girls who like to paint,

sculpt, sing, act, dance, and just play! The great thing

about makeup is that *you can always wash it off,* so grab

a brush and get busy!

outrageous SUZANNE

Face Red face paint streaked under eye.
Eyes Green and blue eye shadow dotted above and below pupils (see p. 58).
Lips Gray lipstick.

At first, I had no intention of doing a **way-out-rageous** look on sweet Suzanne, but after I spent a little time with her, Suzanne showed the **outrageous** side of her personality, and I couldn't resist! I quickly transformed her **cool** look first applying a gray color to her lips. Then I painted a sweep of red face paint (face and body paint are available at most craft or beauty suppy stores) with a paintbrush just under her eye. She looks a little bit **tribal**, and a little bit **space-age**.

outrageous SARAH

Kryolan Aquacolor body and face paint.

The girls and I had a **blast** doing the photos for these looks. I came up with lots of the **ideas** for their makeup by getting to know a little about their **personalities**. For this picture of Sarah, it was late in the day, it was cold, and I was losing the light I needed for her photo. I quickly transformed Sarah by stenciling her. I placed a **stencil** against her skin and sprayed some colored hair spray onto the stencil (*Be very careful* to keep this away from your eyes and nose and to hold your breath while spraying.) You can use the stencils that you find in an **art** supply store, or you can create some by making paper **cut-outs**. I then did a **swipe** of color down one side of her face with a **paintbrush** and some body paint. Once again, take care not to go too close to your eyes. When we were done, Sarah had a sort of **punk**, **graffiti** look—perfect for the cover of a cool **grrrl**-band's CD.

Face Colored hair spray applied carefully and lightly through stencil, swipe of green face paint.
Lips Bright purplish-red lipstick.

outrageous KATRINA

Here is Katrina looking **edgy** and **way-out**. If you want to play with face and body **paint**, get a small paintbrush (about one-to two-inches wide). For this photo, I prepared **blue** and **green** Kryolan Aquacolor by mixing it into a paste with a little water. (This is not always necessary; you can also just wet your **brush** and rub it on the cake of color.) To get Katrina in the mood for this photo, I asked her to pretend that she was a **rock star**. I placed the stencils I had made on her face and neck and brushed the color over them, transforming her previously **glamorous** look into a **way-out-rageous** one. You can do this very quickly and easily on a bare face, or just add the bright color to any makeup you may be wearing. I chose a bold blue and green for Katrina because she is a Scorpio, one of the strong water signs.

Face Green and blue face paint applied with paintbrush.
Eyes See Glamorous Katrina on p. 99.

outrageous DaISY

A ny one of the details we used for Daisy's **way-out-rageous** makeup would look pretty wild **by itself**. We tried lilac cream shadow with very long false eyelashes on one eye. We put a circle of yellow cream shadow around the other eye and small circles of color high on her cheek. If you have great skin, do this without any other makeup or base. Keep the look fresh and pretty by wearing gloss on your lips but no lip color. Have you ever **dreamed** of running away to join the **circus**? Daisy's look has the same sense of **magic** and **fun**—but she didn't have to run away to find it!

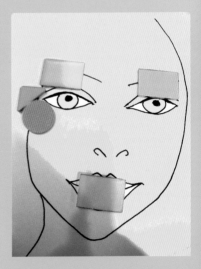

Eyes Lilac cream shadow, false eyelashes on one eye, yellow cream shadow on other eye.
Cheeks Small circles of plum and green cream shadow.
Lips Gloss.

outrageous JENNIFER

Jennifer and her sister Jessica abandoned themselves to all the photo shoots they did for this book, giving themselves **totally** to the different **transformations** and having lots of **fun**. One of my photo shoots with Jennifer spontaneously turned into **freestyle** body **painting**. If you want to **play** with this, first decide on the **colors** that you would like to use. What are your **favorites?** I mixed a few colors of face paint into a thick paste, and then with three different-sized paintbrushes—taking care not to go near her eyes—I applied strokes of color. Wet your brushes ever so slightly before **dipping** them in the paste, and try out the stroke on your arm to make sure you have enough **makeup** on your brush to get a good **streak** of color. You can put two or three colors on your brush at once by separating the hairs with your fingers and dipping the different parts of the brush into different colors. Jennifer looks like a walking, talking **work of art!**

Face and body
Green, purple, yellow, and blue face and body paint.

outrageous Tania

For skin with a yellow undertone like Tania's, a strong contrasting **hot pink** lip color coupled with an unusual eyeliner will look **vibrant** and **way-out-rageous**.

For this makeup, first we applied base, powder, and concealer.

Then we applied a light pink powder eye shadow to the eyelids and a deep shimmery violet in the crease, then winged the violet color upward and outward. We wet an eyeliner brush and applied a thin line of pink liner to the very base of the lashes in the outer corner of the eyes.

We slightly lightened the top of the cheekbone with a little white powder to accentuate them, and then blended warm-colored blush just under the white. When we were done, Tania looked **electric** enough to light up a room!

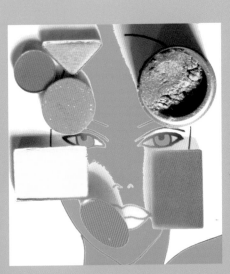

Face Base, powder, and concealer.
Eyes Light pink powder shadow, shimmery violet shadow, pink eyeliner at very base of lashes in outer corner.
Cheeks White powder, warm colored blush.
Lips Hot pink lipstick.

star power

There are nine beautiful, unique planets in our solar system, and there are more stars in the sky than we can count, just as there are all different kinds of beauty and more ways to express that beauty than anyone could number. Are you creative? Strong? Mysterious? Funny? All of the above? Star power is about showing people your own unique galaxy of beautiful qualities—look up your astrological sign, and you'll find a list of colors, traits, and other fun details that make you different from anybody else in the zodiac! You can also read about your friends' signs. Take some of the colors and details that attract you to a different sign and mix them into your own "look" to take your star power to a whole new level!

capricorn

December 24 –
January 20

**Capricorn
Celebrities**
Kate Moss, Safron,
Jude Law, David
Bowie, Jim Carrey,
Diane Keaton,
Elvis Presley, Sissy
Spacek, Tiger Woods
Colors Black, gray,
dark green, navy
Flowers Pansy,
onions, hemlock, ivy
Stone Dark sapphire

Self-contained **Capricorn**, you have expressive features and great cheekbones. Make your beautiful **melancholic** eyes even more **captivating** by accentuating them with blue—right next to the base of the upper and lower lashes and inside the lower rim of the eyes.

Make sure to apply shadow and liner in an outward, but not upward, direction. (Don't start the line *between* the inner corner and the iris, start at the inner corner. This will elongate the eyes.) Capricorn, you tend to have a narrow face shape, and this style of eye makeup will make your eyes appear wider. Do not apply liner and shadow in an upward direction because that could make your face look longer. The same advice goes for blush application.

Define your **lips** lightly with a classic muted pink, and deepen them with black tinted gloss.

crush

Is the guy you want to attract a Capricorn?
Stay sweet and innocent. Wear the softer Taurus colors or the more subdued Pisces look.

aQUaRIUS

January 21– February 18

Aquarius Celebrities
Justin Timberlake, Jennifer Aniston, Christie Brinkley, Stockard Channing, Matt Dillon, Mia Farrow, Farrah Fawcett, Yoko Ono, Chris Rock, Oprah Winfrey, Alicia Keys
Colors Gray, indigo, electric blue, pastels, amber
Flower Orchid
Stone Amber, sapphire, black pearl

Aquarians either have a round face and a large jaw or the opposite—a large forehead and a tapering chin (a triangular face shape). You have large, roundish beautiful eyes and your other features are beautiful, too. You are a cool, distant, creative **beauty**—you often have lots of freckles, and you look great in cool tones, even if you have red hair.

A **monochromatic** (same color on lips, eyes, and cheeks) **pink** makeup will gently enhance your features. If you want to kick it up a notch, accentuate your eyes with **smoky** matte shades of violet, blue, and gray and keep your lip color soft and cool. If **drama** is your goal, a deep violet or gray lip color will do the trick.

You are willing to try anything, and you look great with unusual makeup. You could also warm up your cool beauty by wearing a russet lip color and soft browns on your eyes. Amber jewelry would be effective, too.

crush

Is the guy you want to attract an Aquarius? He will be intrigued by anything unusual, but the feminine, flirtatious Libran makeup or the deep, dark, mysterious Scorpio style are probably your best bets.

PISCES

February 19–March 20

Pisces Celebrities
Drew Barrymore, Kurt Cobain, Cindy Crawford, Fabio, Jean Harlow, Jennifer Love Hewitt, Jon Bon Jovi, Spike Lee, Rob Lowe, Sharon Stone, Elizabeth Taylor, Vanessa Williams.
Colors Purple, turquoise, greenish-blue, silver
Flowers Water lily
Stone Coral, amethyst

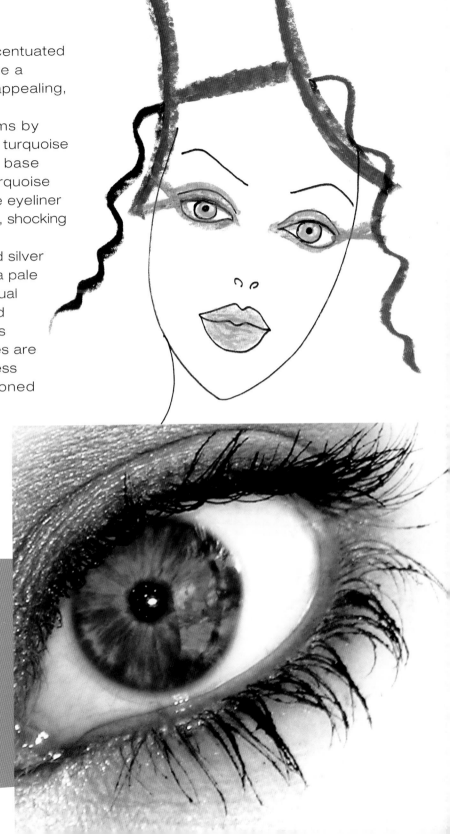

Luminous Pisces, your beauty is accentuated by **cooler** shades. You tend to have a perfect oval **face** that is large and appealing, with melancholic eyes and full lips.

Add to your already **irresistible** charms by emphasizing your melting, watery **eyes** with a turquoise eyeliner pencil inside the lower rim and at the base of the upper lashes. Or, go **wild** and add a turquoise blue shadow in the crease as well and over the eyeliner pencil to strengthen the look further. Use a cool, shocking pink lip color to complete your bold look.

For something more **subdued**, gray and silver are great colors for your eyes. Use them with a pale lilac lip color and shimmery gloss on your sensual lips. Make sure to keep your lovely skin in good condition with moisturizers, and bring out its **glow** with **opalescent** powders. Your features are well-balanced and well-shaped, and the softness of your face allows you to use darker, blue-toned lip colors for a dramatic look. Wear these without eye makeup or with just a thin line of eyeliner to define the almond shape of your eyes, and you've got another gorgeous, easy look.

crush

Is the guy you want to attract a Pisces? He will be attracted by the strength of the Scorpio makeup or by one of the more grounded earth signs, such as a distant, cool Capricorn or an intriguing Virgo.

aries

March 21– April 20

Aries Celebrities
Victoria Beckam,
Ewan McGregor,
Matthew Broderick,
Celine Dion, Sarah
Jessica Parker,
Mariah Carey
Colors Red, gray,
black
Flower Honeysuckle
Stone Bloodstone,
diamond

Dynamic **Aries**, you have great bone structure, a slight aristocratic bump on your nose, and well-shaped lips. Forceful and **modern**, you always get the guy you want, but are you sure you really want him? Always in a hurry, you are often without makeup and look great that way; if you do wear makeup, you tend to find one look and stick with it.

You will find that, surprisingly, if you slow down to take a minute to play with makeup, you will enjoy the **fun** of it and the **attention** it will bring you.

You could try hiding your **strength** with very feminine makeup. Soften your sensuous lips with pale pink lip color and lots of lip gloss (although you do look **fab** in bright red lipstick), and enlarge your **piercing** eyes by combining smoky brown and gray shadows and blending them from your lash line upward past the crease. Then line your eyes with black pencil. Accentuate your great cheekbones with shine by applying a cheek gloss.

A quick and equally effective look is to use one product for all: apply a little soft cream blush or soft gold to each feature—lids, cheeks, and lips.

crush

Is the guy you want to attract an Aries? Aries boys have strong hunting instincts, so you must appear totally unobtainable to get his interest. Try the distant Aquarian look or the smoldering Scorpio.

taurus

April 21 – May 21

Taurus Celebrities
Kirsten Dunst, David Beckam, George Clooney, Audrey Hepburn, Janet Jackson, Michelle Pfeiffer, Uma Thurman, Andy McDowell
Colors Green, pink
Flowers Rose, poppy, violet, foxglove, vine
Stone Emerald

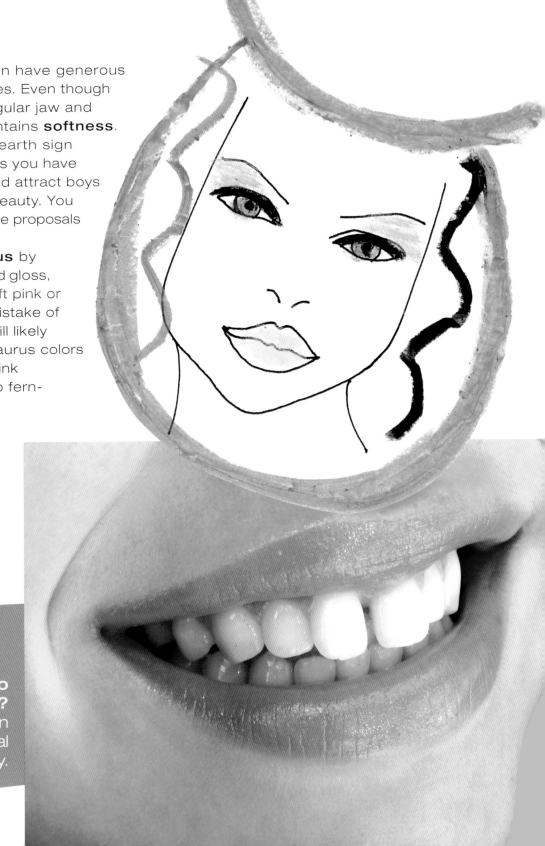

Taurus, you most often have generous features and large eyes. Even though you have a rather angular jaw and cheekbones, your face still maintains **softness**. Extremely sensual, you are an earth sign governed by Venus, which means you have your feet firmly on the ground and attract boys like flies with your **smoldering** beauty. You will probably receive more marriage proposals that any other sign in the zodiac.

Become really **dangerous** by deepening your lips with black tinted gloss, then lighten the center with a soft pink or nude lip color. Don't make the mistake of using a pink foundation, which will likely your large eyes by using your Taurus colors of pink and green; apply a soft pink over the entire eyelid and a deep fern-green in the crease. You could also make them more **exotic**, by blending black shadow around them at the base of the lashes and lining the lower rim of the eye with a black kohl pencil liner.

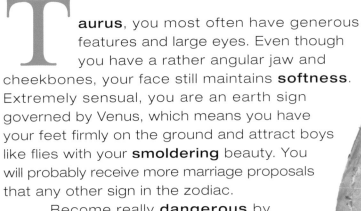

crush

Is the guy you want to attract a Taurus? Try wearing the Libran makeup, which will appeal to his love of beauty.

GeMINI

May 22 – June 21

Gemini Celebrities
Elizabeth Hurley, Colin Farrell, Courtney Cox, Johnny Depp, Nicole Kidman, Paul McCartney, Marilyn Monroe, Isabella Rossellini, Brooke Shields, Jewel, Mary-Kate and Ashley Olsen
Colors Yellow, multicolor mixtures, violet
Flower Lily of the Valley, lavender
Stone Aquamarine, alexandrite

No one is ever bored with the **lively**, intelligent **Gemini**. You are usually **blessed** with good skin, a high forehead, well-balanced features, and great cheekbones. Enhance your feminine, **flirtatious** personality and fabulous almond-shaped eyes by blending a lilac shadow over your eyelids, then applying violet eyeliner to the base of the upper lashes, extending the line to the outer corner of the eyes. Add a pinch of lip color and lots of opalescent gloss to the lips. Soften the angles of your face by just using a soft shade of blush on the apples of your cheeks.

You also look great when you emphasize the **original** side of your personality with a strong black eye makeup or an unusual lip color, such as yellow. With your **mercurial** Gemini personality, you will keep desiring **change**, and that's okay—your features and personality allow you to easily carry off all the makeup in the zodiac, so have fun!

crush

Is the guy you want to attract a Gemini? Drive him crazy with curiosity by being a different girl every time he sees you. Wear the conservative cool Capricorn look one evening, and then the sensual Taurus look the next.

CANCER

June 22–July 22

Cancer Celebrities
Courtney Love, Tobey McGuire, Princess Diana of Wales, Prince William, Ginger Rogers, Missy Elliott, Jessica Simpson, 50 Cent, Meryl Streep

Colors White, pale gold, all pearlescent colors, violet, turquoise

Flowers Acanthus, wildflowers

Stone Opal, moonstone, pearl, crystal

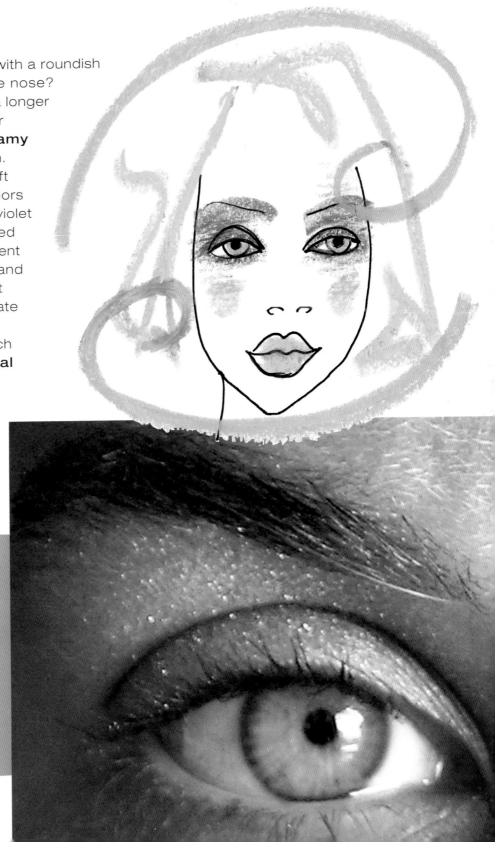

Are you a **full-moon Cancer**, with a roundish face and a short, slightly wide nose? Or are you a half moon, with a longer nose and stronger features? Whichever you are, you probably have a soft, **dreamy** appearance and a luminous complexion. **Capricious** Cancer, bring out your soft lunar **mystery** with lots of pearlized colors around your eyes. Apply a shimmering violet to your lids, then add a touch of pearlized turquoise on top. Sweep on an opalescent blush. Finish the look with pink lip color and a touch of white pearl gloss to highlight your pouty lips. You could also accentuate your highly **creative** nature by using a more unexpected shade of lip color, such as a bright orange. You are **sentimental** and sensitive, but oh my! How you hold onto things. No boy will ever escape you. But then again, why would he want to escape such a devoted, **captivating** creature?

crush

If the guy you want to attract is a Cancer, be mysterious and wear Scorpio makeup (without the dark lipstick), or intrigue him with the style of a cool Capricorn. You could also wear the Gemini makeup; he'll love those violets!

leo

July 23– August 23

Leo Celebrities
Madonna, Ben Affleck, Antonio Banderas, Melanie Griffith, Whitney Houston, Mick Jagger, Jennifer Lopez, Jacqueline Kennedy Onassis
Colors Gold and other metallic colors, rich reds and purples, royal colors
Flower Sunflower, marigold, rosemary
Stone Ruby, diamonds

The strong, radiant beauty of **Leo** the **lioness** stems from your love for life and your **regal** bearing. Your radiant, **confident** beauty attracts many ardent admirers. This will be especially so if you show the world your **warm,** extravagant nature by enhancing your lips with a **vivid** red lip color softened by a dot of pink iridescence in the center. Your beautiful, round, upturned eyes are full of expression and only need slight emphasis. You can do this with a gray or silver shadow near the eye and a light, almost white shade on the brow bone. Black eyeliner emphasizes your eyes well, too—wear it with a pale lip color or just lip gloss. Your rectangular face needs very little, if any, blush, so just highlight your cheekbones with **gold** blush or accentuate your **extravagant** nature with a splash of silver metallic color over one side of your face.

crush

If the guy you want to attract is a Leo, he needs a glamorous woman he can cuddle up to and also protect. If you wear the Sagittarius makeup, you will certainly attract his interest, and the Cancer makeup will bring out his protective instincts.

VIRGO

August 24–
September 22

Virgo Celebrities
Cameron Diaz,
Keanu Reeves,
Ingrid Bergman,
Queen Elizabeth I
(the Virgin Queen),
River Phoenix,
Jason Priestley,
Claudia Schiffer,
Beyonce Knowles
Colors Navy blue,
muted greens,
gray, turquoise
Flowers
Cornflowers, any
small, brightly
colored flowers
Stone Topaz,
aquamarine

eware: a **Virgo** is not as neat and tidy as everyone thinks, and she can be quite crazy at times. A typical Virgo has a soft, oval face, delicate features, and slightly protruding eyes framed by high, delicate eyebrows—but she can still have a hint of wildness. Virgo, you look great in well-**balanced** makeup in warm earthy tones, but break the mold and show your **creativity** and **adventure** by adding touches of color. Apply a sandy yellow to the eyelid, then add touches of a contrasting turquoise in the center of the eye over the pupil. Blend a beautiful brick cream blush over your cheeks and up over the cheekbone to make your face glow. Complete this with a **bold** shade of gloss, such as this brick shade. If you happen to be a Virgo with strong features, like big eyes and lips, give your makeup an **unbalanced** look by wearing only a strong lip color and no eye makeup, try using a soft peachy shade of gloss with a hint of deep-green cream eye shadow.

crush

Is the guy you want to attract a Virgo? Be distant and intriguing. Wear the cool Capricorn makeup or the flirtatious Gemini one. But not the crazy Gemini one, please!

lIBRa

September 23–
October 23

Libra Celebrities
Kate Winslet,
Brigitte Bardot,
John Lennon,
Gwyneth Paltrow,
Susan Sarandon,
Bruce Springsteen,
Sting, Sigourney
Weaver, Eminem
Colors Sky blue,
leaf green, pink,
mustard, black
Flower Rose
Stone Diamond,
white jade, coral

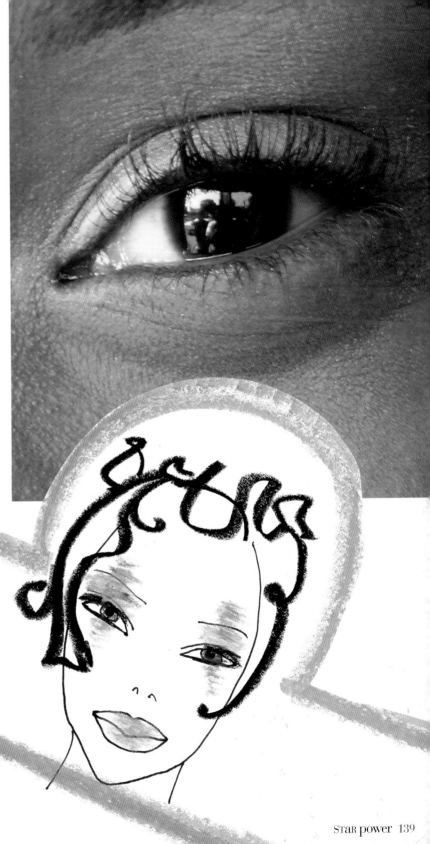

You are governed by **Venus**, the goddess of love. **Elegance** and **refinement** are your two outstanding qualities. **Libras** often have heart-shaped faces, upturned eyes, and beautiful mouths and hair.

You instinctively know how to accentuate and enhance your beauty and are **fascinated** by **color**. Pastels, mustard yellow, and all shades of pink will accentuate your Venusian sensuality and **charm**. You also look enchanting in soft blues. You are gifted with great skills when it comes to makeup and know just how to apply a **dazzling** look like the one in this photo. Pink and yellow are a great combination for you. First apply pink eye shadow, then apply a soft yellow shadow to the inner corners of your eyes. To emphasize your lips, use gloss first, and then outline them **voluptuously** with a brown lip color and a touch of pink. You would also look great with dark, smoky eyes and pale lips.

crush

If the guy you want to attract ia a Libra, remember that a Libra boy is flirtatious and always in love, but it's not so easy to capture his heart. You have to be strong and steady, so try the Aries independent attitude and makeup to catch his eye. He will also love the elegant Libran look.

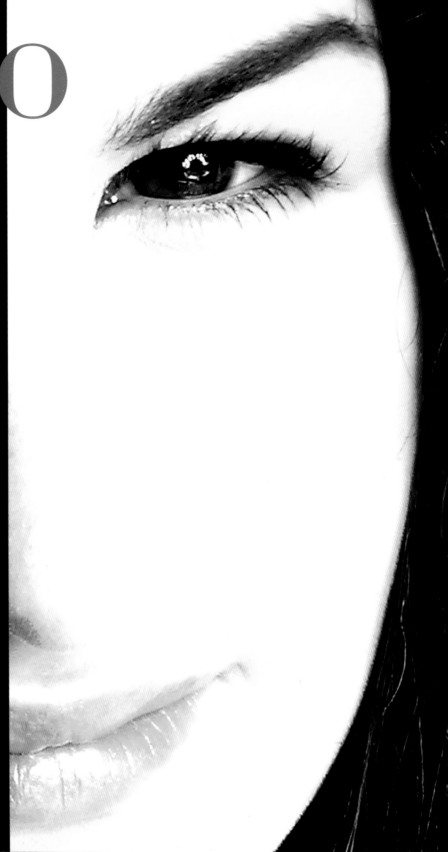

SCORPIO

October 24–
November 22

**Scorpio
Celebrities**
Winona Ryder,
Leonardo DiCaprio,
Jodie Foster, Bill
Gates, Whoopi
Goldberg, Grace
Kelly, Demi Moore,
Meg Ryan, Winona
Ryder, Nelly, Eve
Colors Black,
burgundy, deep
sea green
Flowers
Rhododendron,
dark red flowers
Stone
Bloodstone, topaz

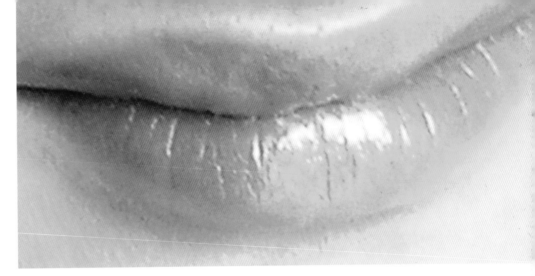

Scorpio, your beauty is **deep** and **mysterious,** and your eyes are totally **magnetic** and piercing. Your coloring is often dark, and you tend have a wide, innocent-looking face. Accentuate your eyes softly by blending a beautiful green shadow over your entire eyelid or by lining the base of your lashes with green. Soften your voluptuous lips with a light gloss.

Although your beauty is strong without makeup, enhancing your features gives you a sense of **power** that you love. If you want to capture someone's heart, only the strongest boy will be a match for your strength (those with any weakness will follow their survival instinct and flee), but if you wear a very deep cream black eye shadow—or almost black with a hint of dark blue or deep sea-green—together with a deep red lip color, you'll be irresistible. Even dark red on your lids with an added dark green pencil in the inner rim of your eyes to increase the **intensity** even further will look fab. With this use a soft peachy shade on your lips, you don't want to go overboard!

crush

If the guy you want to attract is a Scorpio, proceed with caution! He is very tricky, so beware. He is often attracted to more than one girl at a time. Still want to go ahead? Well, then don't overdo it, keep your look elegant. He would probably be attracted by the warmth of the Virgo makeup. The Leo makeup should also do the trick—but lose the silver splash; that might be a little too flashy.

SAGITTARIUS

November 23– December 23

Sagittarius Celebrities
Britney Spears, Brad Pitt, Christina Aguilera, Tyra Banks, Kim Basinger, Maria Callas, Christina Aguilera
Colors Deep blue, purple, orange
Flower Dandelion
Stone Amethyst, turquoise

Your broad angular face has fine, perfect features, which can be easily drowned out, so use makeup delicately. **Sagittarius**, your **joyful**, **sparkling** beauty, wide smile, and **inviting** personality are best enhanced with warm tones. You have, however, an **exciting** edge to your personality, and just using warm tones would be too boring for you. You look best when you accentuate your **edge** by playing with **contrasting colors**. You should always try to keep your skin and cheeks warm and glowing. Your skin is usually **smooth** and even, so a tinted moisturizers is a great way to step up the warmth. To do the contrast well without going overboard, just apply shadow or eyeliner to your eyelids. If you use a warm brown or peach shade on your eyes with lots of mascara, then use a warm orange on your cheeks and a cool shade of pink on your lips. If you wear a cooler shade on your eyes such as a neutral taupe, cool violet, or violet liner (in which you look great) keep your warm orange cheeks and use a **vivid** orange lip color or just a yellow tinted gloss. Try mixing gloss, eye shadow, and a pinch of lip color on your cheeks for the perfect glow just enough to accentuate your sparkling **mischievous** look. "Keep it simple" is a great motto for you.

crush

If the guy you want to attract is a Sagittarius, you'll have your work cut out for you. It is not easy to attract such an adventurous boy—he is always on the move. Try the Aries or Cancer makeup.

Index of Models

alex t.   pp. 4, 10, 37

alice   pp. 9, 10

aziza   pp. 10, 119 (eye, upper left), 138–139

caitlin   pp. 10, 119 (eye, lower left), 124–125

candice   pp. 10, 120–121

daisy   pp. 1, 5, 10, 15 (eyes), 22, 25, 28, 29, 31 (lower right), 49, 61, 69, 115, 132

elizabeth c.   pp. 11, 140–141

elizabeth k.   pp. 11, 29

emma   pp. 11, 29,

esra   pp. 4, 11, 17, 37

jennifer   pp. 6, 11, 62, 101, 116

jessica   pp. 6, 11, 50, 100,

katrina   pp. 5, 11, 46, 60, 70, 81, 89, 98–99, 114, 115

laura   pp. 11, 119 (lips, center), 134–135

lindzay   pp. 12, 17, 122–123

lucinda   pp. 12, 40 (bottom row), 74–75, 84, 92, 105

malaya   pp. 7, 12, 21

marcella   pp. 12, 25, 136–137

melissa   pp. 12, 142–143

ming   pp. 4, 12, 35

natalie   pp. 12, 37

sarah l.   pp. 13, 30 (eyes), 130–131

sarah y.   pp. 12, 41 (top row), 52, 63, 73, 83, 88, 102–103, 113

sasha   pp. 5, 13, 128–129

sky   pp. 13, 31

stephanie   pp. 13, 126–127

suzanne b.   pp. 1, 13, 45, 59, 68, 80, 91, 97, 112

tania   pp. 7, 13, 14 (center: top and bottom), 41 (center row), 54, 64–65, 76, 85, 90, 109, 117,